THE CHRISTIAN UNDERSTANDING OF GOD TODAY

TRINITY COLLEGE, DUBLIN: STUDIES IN THEOLOGY

The Christian Understanding of God Today

THEOLOGICAL COLLOQUIUM
ON THE OCCASION OF THE 400TH
ANNIVERSARY OF THE FOUNDATION OF
TRINITY COLLEGE, DUBLIN

Edited by
James M. Byrne

THE COLUMBA PRESS
DUBLIN 1993

First edition, 1993, published by
THE COLUMBA PRESS
93 The Rise, Mount Merrion, Blackrock, Co. Dublin, Ireland

Cover by Bill Bolger
Origination by The Columba Press
Printed in Ireland by
Colour Books, Dublin

ISBN: 1 85607 087 5

Contents

Foreword, *Sean Freyne* 7

1. The Question of God Today
   Werner G. Jeanrond 9

PART I: *From the Bible to Chalcedon: Problems of Trinitarian Thinking in the Jewish and Christian Traditions*

2. The Emergence of Monotheism in Israel
   Andrew Mayes 26
3. The Naming of God in the Early Christian Experience
   Sean Freyne 34
4. The Nicene Heritage
   Rowan Williams 45
5. The Triune God of Grace: Trinitarian thinking in the theology of the Reformers
   Christoph Schwöbel 49

PART II: *Philosophical and Systematic Reflections on the Christian Understanding Of God*

6. Are there Christian Alternatives to Trinitarian Thinking?
   James Mackey 66
7. Feminist Theology and the Trinity
   Ann Loades 76
8. Some Implications of Cosmology for our Understanding of God as Creator
   Gabriel Daly 81
9. Wittgenstein and the Irrationality of Rational Theology
   Vincent Brümmer 88

PART III: *The Social Implications of the Christian Understanding of God*

10. Some Reflections on the Social Doctrine of the Trinity
Jürgen Moltmann 104
11. The Christian Rhetoric of God and Human Relational Experience
Janet Martin Soskice 112
12. Some Elementary Remarks on the Word 'God'
James M. Byrne 119
13. The Politics of Idolatry
Paul Surlis 130

PART IV: *The Christian Understanding of God in the Context of the World Religions*

14. The Challenge of Interfaith Dialogue to the Christian Understanding of God
Ursula King 138
15. Some Aspects of the Buddhist-Christian Dialogue
David Tracy 145
16. The Trinity in Melanesia: The Understanding of the Christian God in a Pacific Culture
John D'Arcy May 154
17. The Christian God and Allah
Redmond Fitzmaurice 166

The Contributors 173

Foreword

The papers here presented in revised form were first delivered at a conference held in March 1992 to celebrate the Quatercentenary of Trinity College, Dublin. The School of Hebrew, Biblical and Theological Studies, though established as recently as 1980 as a replacement for the Divinity School of the Church of Ireland, is conscious of being heir to a long tradition of theological study. The Regius Chair of Divinity was established as early as 1607 in the very first generation of the College's existence. While many aspects of life at Trinity were celebrated during 1992, our School felt particularly responsible for the celebration of the College's name and founding ethos. Even today there is a decidedly religious flavour to many aspects of its life despite the secular context of the modern university.

Our very successful colloquium, which was attended by more than 100 theologians and theological students from Ireland and abroad over a period of three days, was also open to the increasingly articulate lay, theological public in Ireland. Each night the Edmund Burke theatre was filled to capacity for specially arranged lectures and a panel discussion which presented the most salient points of the colloquium's deliberations to that wider audience. This enthusiastic reception of the many ideas that were expressed has prompted the presentation of these papers now in the belief that they will be of interest to many who are struggling with the issues which our colloquium raised, namely an adequate understanding of the Christian God in the modern world. Hopefully, they will also be of interest to our successors when, a hundred years hence they come to address in their way and with their insights the perennial questions which will, I have little doubt, always find an important place in Trinity's curriculum.

The title of our colloquium, *The Christian Understanding of God Today,* sought to capture the two aspects of the theological task which our School regards as central to its horizons in all our teaching and research. On the one hand there is a body of received tradition which calls for historical study and interpretation in its own right, in the light of the cultural and social assumptions of different key periods as far as the doctrine of God is concerned – Biblical, Early Church, Reformation. Equally, the experience of the modern interpreter and the many challenges that contemporary philosophical, religious and social assumptions pose to the classical notion of God are in need of addressing if an adequate articulation of the Christian understanding of God is to be achieved – adequate that is both to the tradition and the modern worldview. In deciding on the content of the various sessions, we were conscious of the need to operate within the broadest possible methodological framework – inter-disciplinary, inter-church and inter-faith. Only such an approach could hope to capture the many strands of contemporary discussion about God and provide the kind of map that anybody interested in theological discourse requires in order to plot their way through what might otherwise appear to be a forest or a wasteland, depending on one's point of departure.

The thanks of the School are due to all those who made our colloquium such a stimulating experience. It would not have been possible to assemble such a number of distinguished scholars and participants without the generous help of the Quatercentenary Committee of the College, the British Council and the Goethe Institute, Dublin. One of our own graduates, Dr James Byrne, carried out his editorial task of bringing these papers into a coherent collection with admirable skill and insight.

Sean Freyne
Professor of Theology
Trinity College, Dublin

CHAPTER ONE

The Question of God Today

Werner G. Jeanrond

The celebrations of the 400th anniversary of Trinity College Dublin provide us with a unique opportunity to reflect anew upon the appropriateness of trinitarian thinking in the Christian approach to God. Is trinitarian thinking an essential part of the Christian doctrine of God or is it merely one among many possible ways of speaking about God? In this paper I cannot explore all the possible dimensions of a constructive critique of trinitarian thinking past, present or future. Nor do I want to engage in such a comprehensive review. Rather I wish to offer a number of theological observations and questions designed to highlight the context in which our contemporary discussion of the concept of God takes place and to explore to what extent trinitarian language can help us to talk responsibly about the God of Abraham, Moses and Jesus of Nazareth.

1. Trinitarian thinking in academic theology and in popular piety today

As any Christian preacher will have experienced, the hazardous task of addressing the question of the Trinity on Trinity Sunday often causes a serious dilemma. What is one to say about the doctrine of the Trinity to an ordinary Sunday congregation whose sensibility for trinitarian thinking has never been properly awakened? This experience of homiletic *Angst* with regard to the Trinity, however, stands in stark contrast to the academic eagerness of many theologians today to subscribe to trinitarian thinking with remarkable enthusiasm. Even some of those theologians who have advocated that the Greek metaphysical paradigm needs to be replaced by modern or post-modern paradigms are generally very quick to adopt and promote trinitarian language.[1] The Trinity has become the symbol of Christian faith which is most willing, it seems, to accept new tasks of signification. On the one hand, this development may be greeted with approval by those people who are happy whenever any traditional expression of Christian faith is confirmed. Yet it seems, on the other hand, that precisely this kind of people will ultimately be most disappointed when they discover the full spectrum of speculation now invested by theologians in trinitarian language. Liberationist projects, feminist concerns, environmental agendas, social programmes, psychological and other insights are all projected onto trinitarian discourse in theology. And this project tends to transform the trinitarian heritage into quite a different reality than the one envisaged by the original promoters of trinitarian language, i.e. the 3rd and 4th century Christian Fathers.

In order to avert further confusion between an old name from a very different tradition of theological reasoning and new ways of discussing the Christian understanding of God today we have to travel the longer road of exploring what we mean when we refer to God today. Any predilection for one or other particular expression of the reality of God which is not backed by critical moves of retrieval and suspicion would amount to a short-cut and lead to further confusion. In view of these observations it seems to me to be a promising undertaking first to identify more closely the developments and changes in the trinitarian understanding of God and then to assess the measure of suitability of trinitarian language as the best mode of theological expression of our experiences of God today. In other words, even the Trinity as a symbol which gives expression to our experiences of the God of Jesus Christ requires critical attention. The widespread inability of Christians today to relate to this concept should alert theologians to the magnitude of the task which faces them if they wish to commend a trinitarian answer to the major contemporary questions about God.

2. Different forms of trinitarian language

In one way or another some trinitarian formulas have been instilled very firmly into every Christian believer since his or her baptism. The sacramental life and the prayer life of all practising Christians is full of references to the Trinity, or rather to God the Father, Son and Holy Spirit. Few Christians experience the urge to engage in divine algebra or have the time to develop theories of how each one of these three persons in the Trinity is to be related to the other two. Trinitarian speculation has always been seen as belonging to the province of theologians who have taken it as one of their tasks to analyse the conceptual implications and inner coherence of the Christian experiences of God, especially, though not only, at times when the Christian faith needed to be defended against real or assumed enemies from outside or inside the Christian church.

When one looks at the development of trinitarian doctrine from that perspective it is important to appreciate that this doctrine is the result of the particular theological, ecclesiological, social, philosophical, hermeneutical, linguistic, cultural and political contexts of Christian faith in the 3rd and 4th centuries. The biblical texts themselves are neither explicitly trinitarian in their understanding of God, nor are they Nicene or Chalcedonian in their expression. On the contrary, explicitly trinitarian reflection does not emerge until some Fathers of the church begin to speak of God in a triadic form and worry about the nature of the relationship between God and Christ. In particular the fourth century debates which centred upon the claim by the Alexandrian priest Arius that Christ though eternal was a creature of God gave rise to an intense controversy which drew in such theologians as Athanasius and the Cappadocian Fathers. Athanasius insisted that the full divinity of Christ, and that included his full participation in God's essence, needed to be defended if we humans were to have any real hope of being saved by God. Thus, while Arius concentrated on the full divinity of God, Athanasius concentrated on the full divinity of Christ. Neither worried too much about the Holy Spirit who is therefore, not surprisingly, only mentioned in passing by the Council of Nicea. Nicea was most concerned to express through its trinitarian formulations the particular nature of the divinity of Christ, and less concerned to engage in the speculation on all three divine members of the Godhead. That speculation was undertaken subsequently by the Cappadocian Fathers. As one of them, Gregory of Nazianzus, put it:

> For us there is one God, for the Godhead is One, and all that proceeds from Him (i.e., the Father) is referred to the One, though we believe in Three Persons ... there are Three whom we worship.[2]

I would like to stress two aspects of this statement, one is its reference to persons, and the other is its reference to Christian worship. Beginning with the reference to worship it is useful for us today to remind ourselves of the fact that the promoters of trinitarian language in the patristic period were responding theologically to a spiritual and liturgical praxis. Christians experienced God's presence in different ways and were responding to God's presence by addressing different personae of the same God. This word 'person' which for us today means an autonomous human agent with certain rights and duties, did not mean the same in Greek. Rather for Gregory and his Cappadocian friends, *prosopon,* that is the original Greek term which was translated into Latin as *persona,* referred to the mask which an actor wears on stage. Thus, by calling the presence of God in the Father, Son and Spirit a *prosopon* or *persona,* the trinitarian theologians in the early church said positively that God can be and has been experienced in different ways, but also that no such experience would ever be able to reveal the fullness of God's essence. Likewise, the Council of Nicea had also only insisted on the divinity of Father, Son and Spirit without attempting to grasp what this divine essence consists of. Hence, it would be fair to say that the early trinitarian speculations stressed the fact of God's presence in the world and the fact of the plurality of its ways, while at the same time they insisted that the essence of God remains incomprehensible.[3] As such they could rightly claim to operate within the context of biblical theology, since already in the Book of Exodus, Yahweh God is identified by his promise of continuous presence, but apart from that perceived to remain mysterious to human beings (cf. Exodus 3).

Since the social, linguistic and philosophical context in which trinitarian thinking flourished and achieved its purpose in the early church is no longer ours, and since our anthropological and christological concerns have also been radically transformed especially during the last two centuries, we have to re-examine whether it is still in our best interest to continue to use trinitarian language today, and if so under what terms. James P. Mackey has drawn our attention to this question very forcefully when he reminded us in his book *The Christian Experience of God as Trinity,* that it is by no means clear that the development of trinitarian doctrine was a necessary development prescribed by the biblical texts, nor that the treatment of the Spirit in our trinitarian heritage has always been clear or persuasive. Even on its own metaphysical premises the distinctions between the three realities *(hypostases)* in the Trinity remain problematic, and the test case for this set of problems is the unclear understanding of the origin and role of the Holy Spirit.[4]

Christian theologians in the West have reacted in different ways to the challenge of coping with this trinitarian heritage. Today, there are roughly speaking two groups of theologians, namely those who concentrate in their work very firmly and explicitly on trinitarian thinking, and those who examine the concept of God without immediate reference to the traditional trinitarian discourse on God or its lasting potential. Some theologians pay only lip service to the trinitarian character of their theology and never mention the Holy Spirit in their reflections on God, concentrating instead exclusively on the nature of the relationship between God and us and on how this relationship has been transformed by Jesus of Nazareth. One wonders if the explicit affirmation of the Trinity by these thinkers serves only as an indicator that they wish to be considered orthodox by their colleagues and their church leaders in spite of their often radical and fruitful explorations into the concept of God and the communicative problems associated with our reflection upon God.

The second group of theologians is more complex. Among the theologians who engage explicitly in trinitarian reflection are those who continue to think in Greek metaphysical terms and who have no problem with the general inability of most contemporary Christians to relate to God as three persons in one divinity. The radical change in meaning of the word 'person' does not bother them and they see no need for any revision of the classical formulations in trinitarian theology. One would be justified in diagnosing here a certain trinitarian fundamentalism. Among theologians engaged in explicit trinitarian reflection today are those who re-interpret trinitarian thinking by stressing the 'social dimension' of the Trinity and those who feel that any theology which is not altogether trinitarian is not altogether decent Christian theology. They, though for very different reasons from the trinitarian fundamentalists whom I have mentioned, would hold that the Trinity is the most distinctive doctrine of Christian faith and the only authentic way of speaking about God.

For theologians like myself, who are trying to explore the potential of trinitarian thinking in terms of expressing our most distinct experiences of the God of Abraham and of Jesus Christ, a question mark must be placed against any effort, old or new, to offer a comprehensive formula for God's creative and redemptive work, and there is also a troubling uncertainty in terms of the traditional understanding of the Holy Spirit which is taken for granted by the explicitly trinitarian theologians. In view of these difficulties, I propose that we focus for a moment on the two constructive proposals mentioned, namely the proposal of a social understanding of the Trinity and the proposal that only the trinitarian starting-point offers an authentic Christian approach to the question of God. Here I can discuss only one representative of each group.

3. The social understanding of the Trinity

Recently, a number of theologians have advocated a social understanding of the Trinity. Most prominently among them figures Jürgen Moltmann. He wishes to go beyond both an understanding of the Trinity which is based on the Greco-Roman concept of God's *substantia* or essence and the effort of grounding trinitarian thinking in the modern notion of the subject, a notion which is now losing most of its credentials anyway in the light of the post-modern critique of the subject as autonomous agent. Instead Moltmann has emphasized the need to understand the Trinity in the context of the biblical story of God's relationship with his creation. Thus, he proposes, as he calls it, 'a trinitarian hermeneutics' according to which we ought to develop an understanding of the Trinity in terms of connections and relations.[5] Moltmann is, of course, ideally prepared to re-examine the doctrine of God in this way because of his earlier studies in which he has insisted that the Christian experience of the God of Jesus of Nazareth demands that we think of God in terms of radical relations, so radical, in fact, that we must speak of God's own suffering which results from his openness to loving involvement with his creation and the accompanying risk of being rejected. God's love becomes especially visible for us in the story of his relationship with his crucified son. For Moltmann, Jesus is the revealer of the Trinity.[6] And we learn about this revelation through reading the New Testament. 'The New Testament talks about God by proclaiming in narrative the relationships of the Father, the Son and the Spirit, which are relationships of fellowship and are open to the world.'[7] Thus, according to Moltmann 'the Christian doctrine of the Trinity proceeds from the concrete and particular history of the Father, Son and Spirit attested [to] in the Bible and leads to the universal revelation of its unity and Godhead'.[8] The Spirit's work in this network of relationships is identified by Moltmann as the mediator of God's action in Christ. Thus, Moltmann can say God has appointed Jesus as the Son through the resurrection from the dead, and that this has happened 'through "the Spirit that sanctifies"'.[9] The Spirit is not a power that emanates from the Father or the Son, but 'a subject from whose activity the Son and the Father receive their glory and their union as well as their glorification through the whole creation, and their world as their eternal home.'[10] This understanding of the Spirit as subject makes it possible for Moltmann to go beyond the old debate between Eastern and Western theologians and church leaders on whether the Spirit proceeds from the Father through the Son, as maintained in the East, or from the Father and the Son *(filioque)* as maintained in the West.

Based on his relational understanding of the Trinity, Moltmann proceeds to develop his 'social doctrine of the Trinity'. He sees the unity of God 'no longer in the homogeneous divine subject nor in the identical divine subject, but in the eternal *perichoresis* of Father, Son and Spirit'.[11] This new understanding of a mutually relational divine community offers for Moltmann also a possibility to take account of liberationist concerns and of the feminist critique of conceptions of domination in God. For Moltmann (as for Leonardo Boff) the Trinity has now become 'our true social programme', and the understanding of the mutual *perichoresis* offers a new way of looking for truly free social relations.[12]

This new proposal for trinitarian speculation deserves our closest attention. It raises important questions such as the following two:

(1) Does such an extensive trinitarian system create a false sense of order in our efforts to search for God's presence in our world today? The absence of a healthy measure of apophatic suspicion and correction is particularly noticeable in Moltmann's understanding of the Spirit. He regrets the sporadic tendency of theologians to collapse into a binitarian understanding of God

which takes seriously only the Father and the Son and analyses their mutual relationship instead of attributing subject status to the Spirit as mediator between the two. While I would agree with Moltmann that the loss of the Spirit dimension in Christian God-talk would be disastrous, I am not so sure that Moltmann's analysis of the career of the Spirit as third person in the Trinity is the only way to read the Bible. I would like to see more discussion of biblical notions of spirit before we claim that there is a certain progress in spirit awareness from Paul to John through the New Testament.[13] Rather than reducing the Spirit in this way to a unifying agent within this speculative notion of God one could reopen the discussion of the diversity both of spirit theologies in the Old and the New Testaments and of Spirit christologies in the New Testament. As Moltmann himself has stressed repeatedly, we must be careful not to read back later doctrine into the Scriptures, otherwise we are in danger of missing vital perspectives for our understanding of God's relationship to us, an understanding which requires continuous critique and self-critique.

(2) My second question relates to Moltmann's concept of a social Trinity. I wholeheartedly agree with him on the need to think about God from the perspective of God's offer of relationship to us. But I do have a difficulty with his notion of the 'divine community' to which we ought to correspond as a human community. In other words, I find it impossible to think of God as 'our social programme' as Moltmann suggests. Of course, for Christian theology God's love is the foundation of all human action. And since the Bible and through Augustine to Rahner and Barth no serious theologian has ever failed to recognise the social implications of the statement that God is love. But referring to the Trinity as our social programme or even as our programme of social personalism or personal socialism[14] seems to me to confuse levels of theological language, namely the level of symbolic representation of God's loving relationship and the necessary subsequent level of reflection upon adequate strategies for Christian praxis in the world. In view of our inability to know anything about God's inner dialogue, I would hesitate to drive our understanding of the concept of the Trinity so far as to deduct appropriate political actions directly from this.[15]

In spite of these criticisms I welcome Moltmann's insistence on the necessity to think of God in terms of dynamic relationships with his creation. The question arises now whether only such a fully organised trinitarian system can provide us with an adequate understanding of God or if other approaches to God which also stress God's relationality can do equal justice to the experiences of Christians from biblical to post-modern times. In other words, are the insights into God's nature offered by trinitarian doctrine more significant than other insights into God's creative and redemptive relatedness?

4. Is the Trinity the necessary starting-point of Christian God-talk?

In his *Systematic Theology* the German theologian Wolfhart Pannenberg offers a very concise recapitulation of the genesis of trinitarian thinking. He acknowledges that neither the New Testament itself nor the Gospel of John show any explicit teaching of trinitarian relations. Rather the development of trinitarian thinking is the result of a complex process of reflection on the Christian experiences of Jesus as Lord. Pannenberg stresses Athanasius' concern when he writes

> The interest in the full divinity of the Son and the Spirit was grounded in the belief that only under this condition could the faithful reach communion with God through Son and Spirit ... However, the confession of the full divinity of Son and Spirit had not yet clarified the relationship between trinitarian teaching and monotheism.[16]

In this situation, Augustine, for instance, attempted to develop the trinitarian dogma on the basis of the previously stated simple unity of God's essence. He then illustrated the trinitarian thinking by drawing a number of psychological analogies in order to show the compatibility between monotheistic and trinitarian thinking.[17] Similarly, Thomas Aquinas in his *Summa Theologiae* proceeded from the reflection on God and his unity to the discussion of the Trinity. Pannenberg is now convinced that such movements from a concept of God's unity to a concept of the Trinity are responsible for the subsequent collapse of trinitarian thinking in the West. Therefore he argues in favour of discussing God's nature from the start in trinitarian terms:

> An argument in favour of the trinitarian doctrine must begin

> with the way in which Father, Son and Spirit appear in the process of revelation and relate to each other.[18]

Thus, Pannenberg diagnoses a logical necessity of arriving at trinitarian thinking in any adequate interpretation of the Christian revelation of God. In this connection he presupposes that the Spirit is understood already in one way, namely as the one who raised Jesus from the dead. The resurrection is thus the work of the Spirit.

Regarding the theological aims of Pannenberg's trinitarian starting point I have no difficulty in agreeing with him that any theological account of the Christian understanding of God needs to think in relational terms from the beginning. The God whom Jesus proclaims as *Abba,* as near and as loving and inviting is a relational God. And that we must try to give a rational account of this relationality in our theologies is self-evident. But what is not self-evident to me after reading Pannenberg's work is that this relational character of our understanding of the God of Abraham, Moses, and Jesus Christ leads by necessity to a well-balanced trinitarian formula. Moreover, as in the case of Moltmann, I am rather wary that certain high-christological assumptions, as well as a number of unexamined attitudes towards the Spirit, are taken for granted and raised above suspicion by identifying them as necessary ingredients of any proper understanding of the Trinity. Thus, the general inability of most of our fellow Christians to relate consciously to the Trinity today may be aggravated further rather than resolved by such approaches to trinitarian thinking. Again, their emphasis on God's essential relationality is most welcome, but their rationalistic proposals of defining God's essence as relational, though without any hesitation still in the framework of an often unexamined traditional language, appear to me to be too quick a move. Therefore, in the last section of this paper I wish to review some of the situations and expressions in which one can also raise the question of God in today's world and language in addition to the trinitarian matrix.

5. The Question of God Today

In this century we have seen some significant re-examinations of both our human self-understanding and its religious dimensions. These re-examinations were provoked in part by the emergence of a new philosophical paradigm according to which only knowledge based on human experience can be recognised as authentic, and in part by the accumulation of insights into the radical ambiguity and plurality of our human condition.[19]

Anybody who takes seriously these forceful insights into the plurality and ambiguity of our human condition will naturally be careful not to subscribe uncritically to any one particular formula or system which promises a total rationality for a particular understanding of God and the human self. God has been invoked too often by people of sinister intentions, but much worse, God has also been cited to cover appalling acts by people of genuinely good intentions. Taking the history of our century seriously requires an enormous amount of suspicion against our most cherished beliefs, assumptions and claims, especially with regard to what is considered to be most sacred. The cries of the victims of racism and totalitarianism in Auschwitz, the victimization of women which is still continuing, the ecological exploitation of the world, the warfare between peoples, partly at least for religious reasons, the political, cultural, and economic exploitation of third world countries and peoples; these and similar experiences are all part of the context in which we raise the question of God again today. Since all religious symbols and systems, including the Trinity, can be used and often have been used at some stage to justify the destruction of human relationships and the physical or spiritual extinction of women, men and children, we may be forgiven for being less enthusiastic to subscribe too quickly to any theological formula, framework or system such as the trinitarian one.

In view of the Enlightenment emphasis on experience and the accompanying development of historical consciousness, we have become more and more aware that the second person of the Christian Trinity, Jesus Christ, had himself a Jewish history and a Jewish experiential background that reaches far beyond the grasp of any trinitarian formula interested predominantly in the divine Logos in Christ. That means, our christological debates, especially in the last three decades, have allowed us to appreciate anew that Jesus proclaimed in fact nobody other than Yahweh God, the God of Israel, and his reign; and that is the God known and worshipped because of his loving and caring presence and because of his unceasing efforts to restore the covenant between his people and him, that covenant which has so often been broken.

Moreover, recent discussions of pneumatology have uncovered the great plurality of ways in which Jesus, his ancestors, his fellow-believers in Israel, and subsequent generations of Jews have referred to the Spirit-presence of God, be it as *ruach,* as wisdom, as wind or even as storm.[20]

Similarly, the intensified dialogue with other world religions has taught us Christians that we are not the only religious tradition which sees God in relational terms and which has experienced God through his many spiritual manifestations. Who would want to deny the relationality of Allah and the relational quality of Hindu or Buddhist experiences of the sacred? We Christians therefore are not in a position to claim an exclusive insight into God's relational character. But what we can rightly claim is our commitment to develop non-dominating and loving relationships in response to our experience of God's love for us.

Thus, it would appear that any trinitarian concept of God would need to be explored much further and tested in terms of its continuing adequacy to express our experiences of God's presence. We must resist any effort to force any new religious and theological insight into a conceptual straight-jacket, if we genuinely wish to remain open to further surprising experiences of God's presence in our world. Hence I would be very careful not to declare too hastily that the concept of the Trinity offers enough space for any new christological, pneumatological or feminist critique of traditional theology and of images of God and Christ.

Our knowledge of God's presence and love must, however, be complemented by our admission of God's mysterious nature. Eberhard Jüngel reminded us that mystery does not mean the same as secret.[21] God is not playing secretive games with us; rather God invites us to remain open to his mysteriously unfolding presence. This openness to God's surprising activity requires a theology which is at the same time affirmative and negating. As David Tracy has forcefully stressed, we need to balance our Christian eagerness to say all that we know about God with the experiences of our own and other mystical traditions of the 'Hidden-Revealed-Comprehensible-Incomprehensible-always-

Greater God'.[22] Hence, we are in need of paying renewed attention to the surprises of God's manifestation in our own midst, i.e. in creation and incarnation, instead of concentrating all of our theological efforts in the designing of new schemes of Christian doctrine and their proclamation. Only a revisionist method, i.e. a theological method which is prepared constantly to review itself and the tradition, can protect Christian theology from such doctrinal hubris.

We are no longer searching for the ontological stability which our ancestors in the Early Church looked for, nor are we obsessed with schemes of individual forgiveness in the same measure as our medieval brothers and sisters were. Paul Tillich once described our generation as a generation longing for meaning, longing to understand the purpose of our lives in this universe and the mysterious plan of this cosmos as a whole.[23] Thus, we will never be satisfied with the proclamation of a God who guarantees mere being, nor with a God who offers only individual salvation from eternal punishment. We late twentieth century people have become aware of the dangers of logocentrism and the pitfalls of a reduction of Christian faith to a mere insurance policy for our personal eternity. Rather we are restlessly searching for God in all areas of our cosmos. We follow God's traces not only in traditionally religious spheres, but also in science, in the arts, in literature, music, nature, and most of all in the encounter with the other human being and the other in our own selves. We are determined to exclude no space, time or language from this search for God.

Traditional religious language and secular language alike have therefore become the objects of theological reflection today. Both resources for our thinking are equally suspect and promising, and both need to be assessed according to their potential for transforming our relationships with each other, ourselves and God. This search for God's Spirit in this world and for his reconciling and transforming power is thus unlimited. As Christians we have found orientation for this search from our reflection on God's action in Israel, in Jesus Christ and in the Christian movement. But we cannot afford to limit our search only to our story with God, to our set of past experiences. Once one has received a compass, one has not yet travelled the world, but one is prepared to travel. Theological reflections will have to be measured according to their appropriateness in guiding us in this restless, though exciting journey, and they will have to be re-examined, confirmed, corrected and transformed according to our best critical insights on the way.

6. Conclusion: The Potential of Trinitarian Thinking

In these introductory observations on the question of God today, I have tried to show that trinitarian thinking has a history and represents one promising way of assuring that God's essential relationality is not forgotten in Christianity. But such a reminder can function best, when the language itself in which it is expressed does not become an object of sacred devotion. Trinitarian language, as we have seen, can function exclusively and inclusively. By this I mean that the doctrine of the Trinity can be used as a way of establishing boundaries of superior knowledge against other forms of adequate Christian theological discourse and against the quest of other religious traditions, especially Judaism. But trinitarian language can also be used inclusively, and that means as an affirmation of God's loving presence in Jesus Christ and in other realms of this cosmos. One of the great legacies of trinitarian thinking has been, as we saw from our brief look at the Cappadocian Fathers, that their understanding of God as a Trinity of persons pointed already to the mysterious nature of God, a mystery which is inviting and open to everybody eager to participate in its relational praxis, a genuine mystery which will only reveal itself more fully to those who participate in such a praxis of love.

Notes

1. 'The remarkable resurgence of interest in a trinitarian understanding of God for Christian self-understanding in the last twenty years is not occasioned only by a rediscovery of traditional resources in theology. Rather, the new debate on how to construe God's reality in trinitarian terms can prove to be either very modern (e.g. Hegelian) or anti-modern – i.e. anti-liberal theology – (e.g. Barth or von Balthasar) or post-modern (e.g. in aspects of the thought of Jean-Luc Marion).' David Tracy, 'The Hermeneutics of Naming God', *Irish Theological Quarterly* 57 (1991) 257.

2. Gregory of Nazianzus, *Oration* 31 [On the Holy Spirit] 14. This

translation from Thomas Hopko, 'The Trinity in the Cappadocians', in Bernard McGinn and John Meyendorff, eds., *Christian Spirituality*, vol.1: *Origins to the Twelfth Century* (New York: Crossroad, 1988) 265.

3. Cf. James P. Mackey, *The Christian Experience of God as Trinity* (London: SCM, 1983) 145, stresses the apophatic and mystical tendencies of this approach to God as Trinity.

4. Cf. Ibid. esp. 135-63.

5. Jürgen Moltmann, *The Trinity and the Kingdom of God* (London: SCM Press, 1981) 19.

6. Ibid. 65.

7. Ibid. 64.

8. Jürgen Moltmann, *History and the Triune God* (London: SCM Press, 1991) 82.

9. *The Trinity and the Kingdom of God* , 87.

10. Ibid. 126.

11. *In the History of the Triune God*, xii.

12. Ibid. xiii.

13. *The Trinity and the Kingdom of God* , 125.

14. See Moltmann's contribution to this volume, chapter 10.

15. See here also the critical questions raised by Alistair McFadyen, 'The Trinity and Human Individuality: The Conditions for Relevance', *Theology* 95 (1992) 10-18.

16. Wolfhart Pannenberg, *Systematische Theologie*, vol.1 (Göttingen: Vandenhoeck & Ruprecht, 1988) 298.

17. Ibid. 309.

18. Ibid. 325.

19. See for further details David Tracy, *Plurality and Ambiguity: Hermeneutics, Religion, Hope* (San Francisco: Harper & Row, 1987).

20. See *We Believe in the Holy Spirit. A Report by the Doctrine Commission of the General Synod of the Church of England* (London: Church House Publishing, 1991).

21. Eberhard Jüngel, Entsprechungen: *Gott – Wahrheit – Mensch* (Munich: Kaiser, 1980) 330.

22. 'The Hermeneutics of Naming God', op. cit., 264. Cf. also David Tracy, 'Approaching the Christian Understanding of God', in Francis Schüssler Fiorenza and John P. Galvin, eds., *Systematic Theology: Roman Catholic Perspectives* (Dublin: Gill and Macmillan, 1992) 146.

23. Paul Tillich, *The Courage to Be* (Glasgow: Collins, 1984) 63-8.

PART I

From the Bible to Chalcedon: Problems of Trinitarian Thinking in the Jewish and Christian traditions

CHAPTER TWO

The Emergence of Monotheism in Israel

Andrew Mayes

I

The emergence of Israelite monotheism is to be traced within the historical experience of Israel. That is to say, Israelite monotheism is not to be understood as a religious doctrine originating elsewhere and simply adopted by Israel. The Aten cult in Egypt under Amenophis IV in the 14th century may well have been a monotheistic movement, reflecting a widespread crisis of polytheism at the time, but even if some connection is established between this and Moses, the monotheistic movement in Israel cannot be separated from historical and social developments specific to Israel. Monotheism is more than a religious doctrine.

Israel's historical experience is to be reconstructed from documents which received their final form in the exilic and post-exilic periods, that is, a time when monotheism was established, a time when monotheism was the perspective from which the past was understood, presented and judged. Thus, when the deuteronomistic historian in the books of Joshua, Judges, Samuel and Kings, presents Israel's history as a time of constant falling away from Yahweh, leading to an irretrievable breakdown in the covenant relationship between Yahweh and Israel, it should not necessarily be concluded that a monotheistic idea or ideal was present in Israel from the begining; rather, monotheism is a point of arrival which has supplied the criterion for a retrospective and anachronistic judgement to be passed on Israel's history.

Perhaps even that, however, is to put things much too strongly. For the fact of the matter is that for Israel monotheism as we now perhaps understand it does not play a very vital role, and insofar as monotheism does appear, its character is very much determined by the characteristics and concerns of Yahwism as it was practised in a polytheistic context. This, it seems to me, gives a particular significance to Israelite monotheism which is of integral importance to it.

Following Theissen, especially, I shall try to explain and illustrate this through three points. First, by showing that Israelite religion in the pre-exilic period was characterized by a tendency towards establishing Yahweh and the relationship between Yahweh and Israel as *exclusive;* secondly, by showing that it was out of the exilic situation that a tendency emerged towards establishing Yahweh as *unique;* thirdly, by illustrating how the understanding of Yahweh's *uniqueness* was influenced by the earlier understanding of his *exclusiveness.*

II

In the period up to 586 BC Yahweh's exclusiveness was established. There are two aspects to this. On the one hand, Yahweh became the God of Israel, and, on the other, Israel became the people of Yahweh. Insofar as these aspects are governed by the notion of exclusiveness they are not simply two ways of saying the same thing. Yahweh became the God of Israel alone, and of no other people, before Israel became a people which worshipped Yahweh alone.

The first aspect is rooted in historical developments that can no longer be reconstructed in detail. Yahweh seems to have been known and worshipped before the rise of Israel, or at the very least we must say that the origins of Yahwism are to some extent independent of the origins of Israel. Israel, to judge even from its name, was originally not a Yahweh but an El worshipping community, which originated within the land of Palestine. Yahweh derives from the southern wilderness outside Palestine (cf. Deut 33:2; Judg 5:4; Hab 3:3), and may have an original connection with the Midianite-Kenites or even with Edom (de Moor, *Rise of Yahwism,* 108ff., points to a possible occurrence of the short form Yw at Ugarit). The introduction of the worship of Yahweh into Israel, perhaps by people who had escaped from slavery in Egypt, is the decisive point from which Yahweh became the God of Israel and of no other people. The reason for this decisive development is probably a conglomeration of influences, many of which must remain unknown. But among the probable known influences we may point to the following: the dominating position in Israel eventually achieved by those who were the carriers of the worship of Yahweh into Israel (Ephraim-Benjamin); the fact that Yahweh was the type of personal God already known in

Israel (patriarchal type of God); the fact that Yahwism expressed an ideology of deliverance, of survival and of hope for the future which offered a means by which the tenuous and uncertain self-understanding and identity of Israel could be strengthened over against its environment.

The relationship of Yahweh to Israel from this point onwards parallels that of Chemosh with the Moabites (cf. Judg 11:24) and of Ashur with the Assyrians: Yahweh is the God of Israel and of no other people. But this does not mean that Israel at this time worshipped only Yahweh. There is some evidence to show that for much of Israel's pre-monarchic and monarchic history the worship of other gods besides Yahweh was to be found. A couple of points are relevant here. First, even if one is to classify early Israelite religion as polytheistic, it was certainly not polytheistic on the scale of Egypt, Mesopotamia or even Ugarit. In these advanced and heterogeneous societies numerous gods reflected and related to the myriad concerns of these societies. In Israel, on the other hand, as in similar more homogeneous newly emergent societies of Syria-Palestine, a national god dominated and tended to assume the characteristics of those few other deities that may have been worshipped. So, Yahweh and El were identified (Yahweh may, indeed, have been considered a manifestation of El from the beginning, not a foreign god who merged with El in Canaan); the cult of the goddess Asherah, who was originally paired with El, has left marginal traces (Gen 49:24-26 'breasts and womb' a title of Asherah; Kuntillet Ajrud; cult stand from Tanaach; cf. Smith, *Early History of God*, 16ff.); only the veneration of Baal seems to have endured as an independent cult.

Secondly, it is probably a distortion to introduce a distinction between popular and official religion into this context. While Yahweh was the national God of Israel, and imagery associated with the worship of other gods was often assimilated to Yahweh, it seems that the veneration of Baal was by no means confined to easily identifiable popular contexts, but was an integral part of the religious spectrum at all levels. Names compounded with Baal appear at leadership levels, and temples for Baal were erected in the capital city. The worship of Baal is a feature of Israelite religious life which cannot either be confined to the lower social levels or explained away as the result of occasional and regrettable Canaanite influence.

It was because Yahweh was the national God of Israel that the demand for his exclusive worship eventually appeared. This can be traced first to the early north Israelite prophets of the 9th century, Elijah and Elisha, and its setting is a quite specific one. It is associated with the attempt made by Ahab and Jezebel in the northern kingdom of Israel to replace Yahweh as Israel's national God with Baal. Here again, this is not to be seen as a defence of Israel against the encroaches of Canaanite Baal worship, but rather as a rejection of specific social developments within Israel associated with Israelite worship of the god Baal.

The demand for the exclusive worship of Yahweh was strengthened by the first of the classsical prophets preaching in the northern kingdom, Hosea and Amos, a demand which is allied with a condemnation of social and economic developments in the nation. The destruction of the northern kingdom by the Assyrians in 721 BC, shortly after the preaching of these prophets, validated their demands and fuelled movements for reform which subsequently appear in the surviving southern kingdom of Judah. A fateful link was established between political crisis and neglect of Yahweh, and this, in the succession of crises which characterised the remaining history of the southern kingdom, ensured the increasing strength and influence of the Yahweh-alone movement and ideology in the years leading up to the destruction of Judah and Jerusalem by the Babylonians in 586 BC.

The worship of Yahweh alone, when eventually established, was not, of course, an expression of monotheism. A more appropriate term is monolatry. The existence of other gods was not denied, and indeed the first commandment of the decalogue, a deuteronomic composition, presupposes their existence. Yahweh was the God of Israel, and his worship was confined to that people and that country. Jephthah, in his territorial dispute with the Moabites or Ammonites, acknowledges this: 'Will you not possess what Chemosh your god gives you to possess? And all that Yahweh our God has dispossessed before us we will possess' (Judg 11:24); this is the presupposition also in David's complaint to Saul: 'If it is Yahweh who has stirred you up against me, may he accept an offering; but if it is men, may they be cursed before Yahweh, for they have driven me out this day that I should have no share in the heritage of Yahweh, saying, 'Go, serve other gods' (1 Sam 26:19).

III

Monotheism emerged in Israel particularly in the thought of the later deuteronomistic school and that of 2 Isaiah. This was an evolutionary as much as it was a revolutionary development, but one should not underestimate the breakthrough it represented. In terms of its particular significance for the time, it was a response to and a way of overcoming the crisis that the events of 586 BC represented for Yahwistic faith. In the defeat of Judah at the hand of the Babylonians Yahweh was showing not his weakness over against the gods of Babylon, but his universal power and direction of history to his own ends. The victory which the Babylonians credited to Marduk was the work of Yahweh who was punishing his people for breach of covenant.

Certainly the presuppositions for exilic monotheism are to be found earlier, particularly in the eighth century prophets. It is in Amos that we find: 'Are you not like the Ethiopians to me, O people of Israel? says Yahweh. Did I not bring up Israel from the land of Egypt, and the Philistines from Caphtor and the Syrians from Kir?'(Amos 9:7); Isaiah likewise proclaims 'Ah, Assyria, the rod of my anger, the staff of my fury! Against a godless nation I send him, and against the people of my wrath I command him' (Is 10:5f.); and in his temple vision this same prophet proclaims of Yahweh: 'the fullness of the whole earth is his glory' (Is 6:3). But the apparent universalism of these words never leads to an explicit monotheism, and is compatible with monolatry, or, indeed, polytheism. Statements such as these are to be interpreted perhaps within the context of the tendency of prayer, even in a polytheistic context, to ascribe all divine powers to the god to whom one turns in supplication (cf. Lohfink, *Great Themes from the Old Testament*, 139ff.). Even Mesha, the king of Moab, said that the reason for the fact that Israel had conquered his country was that 'Chemosh was angry with his land'.

One can trace two stages in the presentation of monotheism in the exilic period. First, and closely related to the pre-exilic universalism of the prophets, there is the assertion that Israel's experience in history does in fact lead to the conclusion that Yahweh alone is God: 'Did any people ever hear the voice of a god speaking out of the midst of the fire, as you have heard, and still live? Or has any god ever attempted to go and take a nation for himself from the midst of another nation, by trials, by signs, by wonders and by war, by a mighty hand and an outstretched arm, and by great terrors, according to all that Yahweh your God did for you in Egypt before your eyes? To you it was shown, that you might know that Yahweh is God; there is no other besides him' (Deut 4:33ff.). Israel's experience is unique; Israel's God is unique. Secondly, 2 Isaiah takes up at the point where Deut.4 leaves off: Israel's historical experience is throughout related to faith in Yahweh as creator: 'Why do you say, O Jacob, and speak, O Israel, My way is hid from Yahweh, and my right is disregarded by my God? Have you not known? Have you not heard? Yahweh is the everlasting God, the Creator of the ends of the earth' (40:27f.); 'I am Yahweh, and there is no other, besides me there is no God ... I form light and create darkness, I make weal and create woe, I am Yahweh, who does all these things'(45:5,7). Again, one may say that Yahweh had been worshipped in earlier time both as lord of history and as creator, but it was only in the exile that this belief was explicitly brought to its monotheistic conclusion.

IV

It was not only in Israel that monotheism emerged at this time (philosophical monotheism appears with Xenophon in Greece), and its appearance in Israel should not be divorced from that broader context: a general transformation in forms of thinking about the sacred seems to have taken place independently in different places. Israelite monotheism, however, remained strongly attached to its roots in Israel, and I should like finally to refer to those elements of discontinuity and continuity which characterize monotheism in Israel.

Discontinuity is clearly shown by a comparison of two passages from Deuteronomy (cf. Braulik), one (Deut 5:9f.) from the pre-exilic context of Israelite monolatry, the other (Deut 7:9f.) from the exilic context of Israelite monotheism. The first is part of the decalogue, and reads: 'I, Yahweh your God, am a jealous God, visiting the iniquity of the fathers upon the children to the third and fourth generation of those who hate me, but showing steadfast love to thousands of those who love me and keep my commandments.' The second is surely a deliberate revision of this: 'Know therefore that Yahweh your God is God, the faithful God who keeps covenant and steadfast love with those who love him and keep his commandments, to a thousand generations, and requites to their face those who hate him, by destroying them; he will not be slack with him who hates him, he will requite him to his face'. In the first, the emphasis lies on Yahweh as a jealous God, a pre-deuteronomic understanding of Yahweh which presupposes the possibility of Israelite worship of other gods, and so belongs in a generally polytheistic context. It is true that jealousy is a frequent attribute of gods in the ancient near east and presupposes polytheism. In Israel's attribution of jealousy to Yahweh, however, there is a particular significance: now it is the national god who is jealous of all other gods; this constituted a threat to polytheism much more serious than the kingship of Amon Re or of Marduk among the gods. No place existed for any meaningful role of other deities in Israel (de Moor, *Rise of Yahwism*, pp.223ff.). In the second passage Yahweh is a faithful and merciful God, and it is his love which is emphasized, a perception of Yahweh which grows out of the struggle to reconcile monotheistic universality with Yahweh's particular covenant relationship with Israel. In the first, Yahweh's angry punishment, which may extend to a fourth generation, is mentioned first; in the second, it is Yahweh's love which may extend to a thousand generations while his punishment is directed only to the wrongdoer. In the first, the covenant relationship is that established at Horeb, and requires Israel's obedience to the law there proclaimed; in the second, the covenant relationship is that which was established with the patriarchs and is based solely on Yahweh's promise.

But if monotheism heralded a transformation of some ways of thinking about Yahweh, there are also strong elements of continuity, and it is here, I suspect, that we find what is distinctively Israelite about Yahwistic monotheism. Israelite monotheism is a protest against polytheism and is consistently allied with a call to repent, to change one's behaviour, to return to Yahweh, a return which is effected by Yahweh himself: 'I will gather them from all the countries to which I drove them in my anger and my wrath and in great indignation; I will bring them back to this place, and I will make them dwell in safety. And they shall be my people, and I will be their God. I will give them one heart and one way, that they may fear me for ever, for their own good and the good of their children after them. I will make with them an everlasting covenant, that I will not turn away from doing good to them; and I will put the fear of me in their hearts, that they may not turn from me' (Jer 32:37ff.; cf. also Jer 24:7; Ezek 11:17ff.). The call for a change of behaviour, which is rooted in the pre-exilic prophets, reaches into the social, economic and political spheres; Israelite religion, even in its monotheistic form, indeed perhaps particularly in its anti-polytheistic monotheistic form, constitutes a fundamental criticism of society. Polytheistic societies, marked by differentiation and conflict between their internal factions, in which each god represents a sphere of life and a set of values and needs, lose their legitimation in a critique in which all areas of life come under the rule of one God: 'Hear, O Israel: The Lord our God is one Lord'(Deut 6:4).

Bibliography

Braulik, G., 'Das Deuteronomium und die Geburt des Monotheismus', *Gott der Einzige* (Herder: 1985) 115-159.

Lohfink, N., 'God: The Polytheistic and Monotheistic Way of Speaking about God in the Old Testament', *Great Themes from the Old Testament* (T.& T. Clark: 1982) 135-53.

'Das Alte Testament und sein Monotheismus', *Der eine Gott und der dreieine Gott,* ed. K.Rahner (München: 1983) 28-47.

Miller, P.D., et al.(eds.), *Ancient Israelite Religion* (Fortress: 1987).

de Moor, J.C., *The Rise of Yahwism,* BETL XCI (Louvain: 1990).

Smith, M., *The Early History of God* (Harper and Row: 1990).

Theissen, G., *Biblical Faith* (SCM: 1984).

CHAPTER THREE

The Naming of God in the Early Christian Experience

Sean Freyne

I would like to approach my topic by addressing the following issue: the naming of God in the early Christian experience. This seems a more promising perspective, not just for avoiding the perennial problem for so much of Christian theology, namely the reading back into our foundational texts of later formulations of doctrines, but also in helping us with our own contemporary efforts to name God adequately. Implicit in such approaches as 'Trinitarian thinking in the New Testament' is the assumption that there was a natural development, whereby later conciliar statements are simply the unfolding of doctrines already present in the earlier texts. Both the historical-critical method and modern hermeneutical theory of retrieval and suspicion, have alerted us to the fact that there is a considerably greater rupture, discontinuity and innovation in the history of Christian doctrine than the traditional account allows for. In addition the recognition in contemporary biblical studies of the importance of the social world for the construction of overlapping, yet varied symbolic universes among early Christians, is something that systematic theologians will have to take into account in their reflections. We simply do not have a single, univocal New Testament understanding of either God or Christ. That situation, relentlessly exposed by the History of Religions approach to early Christianity over the past 150 years, has made the very possibility of a Theology of the New Testament so highly problematical today. We shall have to begin to take the fact of plurality seriously as a theological category as well as an historical reality.

When all that has been acknowledged it still remains true that the early Christian witnesses shared a common pre-text in the Jewish *Shema'*: Hear, O Israel, the Lord your God is one (Dt 6:4). Irrespective of the meaning and function of this declaration within the Deuteronomistic reform, it was made to serve a very specific function in terms of Jewish self-identity in later centuries.[1]

From the hellenistic age onwards the Greek world under the influence of Platonic thought knew of the formula 'one God', but this did not exclude other gods also as intermediaries. Indeed throughout the whole of pagan antiquity, monotheism and polytheism were not regarded as mutually exclusive. Celsus, the second century CE anti-Christian writer, declares that it made little difference whether one called god the Most High, or Zen, or Adonai, or Sabbaoth or Amoun like the Egyptians *(Contra Celsum* V, 45). His contemporary, Maximus of Tyre states that the one doctrine upon which all the world is united in accepting is that 'one God is king of all and Father and that there are many gods and sons of God that rule together with God' (XXXIX, 5).[2]

In such a climate of tolerant monotheism Jewish thinking about God's oneness varied from an acceptance of the current pagan thinking at one extreme – the hellenisers at the time of Antiochus Epiphanes, who were prepared to identify Yahweh with Zeus (2 Macc 6:2), to the sectarian attitudes of the Qumran community at the other, who attempted to exclude Greek influences from their lives altogether. Those who sought the via media, such as Philo and Josephus, were at pains to establish the credibility of the Jewish understanding of God in the pagan environment of Alexandria and Rome.[3] The law of Moses was of universal significance, they argued, thus tapping into Greek cosmological speculation about the relationship of God to the world. The slogan most frequently used became *heis theos* , 'one God' and not *kyrios heis,* 'one lord' of Dt 6:4. Philo in particular shows the possibility of adapting the biblical concept of God to the presuppositions of Greek philosophy, without falling into the trap of the prevailing tolerant monotheism. John Dillon interprets Philo against the background of Middle Platonist discussions about the distinction between the Supreme God, knowable only to those who were capable of true philosophical contemplation, and the Demiurge who creates the physical world and whom Philo identified with the Stoic *logos,* who also could be called God.[4] This second God helps to explain the anthropomorphisms in the Biblical text. Moses knew full well that the supreme God was nameless, 'since it is not the nature of the one who is to be spoken of, but simply to be' (*De Somniis,* 1,230-33). Hence it was to the *logos* that the tetragrammaton, or divine name was given. Yet, despite the best efforts of such Jewish apologists, pagan anti-Judaism continued to see the Jews as intolerant and exclusivist, precisely because of their monotheistic views.

While Jewish thinkers, influenced by the larger hellenistic ethos, were attempting to establish the outer limits of their monotheistic faith within the framework of the *Shema'*, other developments were also taking place that had a bearing on early Christian articulations of their own experience of God. The figure of wisdom active in creation had provided Jews in the homeland (*Ben Sirach*) and in the Diaspora (*Wisdom of Solomon*) with a point of contact with Greek speculation about the world soul, without succumbing to an easy syncretism. In the Targumim we meet the *memra* and the *shekinah* as ways of expressing the divine decrees and the divine presence to Israel.[5] It is sometimes said that these designations resulted from the desire to avoid speaking anthropomorphically of God in early Jewish thought after the Babylonian exile. While there may well be truth in this point of view, on closer examination these expressions help to articulate various aspects of God's activity in the world, particularly availability in the cult and the expression of the divine will for Israel. Even later Rabbinic writings echo some of these contemporary concerns negatively insofar as one repeatedly finds reference in the midrashic and talmudic literature to the heresy of 'the two powers in heaven', possibly reacting not just against Christians and gnostics but also against hellenistic Jews like Philo who appeared to compromise with the contemporary philosophical speculations. Thus a good deal of exegetical energy was expended in showing that the different, even conflicting attributes of God found in different passages of Scripture in no way impaired the oneness of God. As the *Mekhilta of R. Ishmael*, admittedly a rather late document, puts the matter succinctly: 'Scripture would not give an opportunity to the nations of the world to say there are two powers in heaven, but declares : I am Yahweh your God. I was in Egypt, I was at the sea, I was in the past, I will be in the future to come. I am in this world, I am in the world to come.'[6]

It was possible then at least for some Jews to maintain the ancestral monotheistic faith, albeit with the Greek sounding expression that God is one and at the same time engage in the contemporary philosophical discussions about the nature of God and God's relation to the created universe. Consequently, dyadic and triadic patterns of thought are to be found in Jewish circles other than the Christian one, particularly among those, like Philo, who sought to remain open to the larger environment and the issues being discussed there.[7] Hopefully this all-too brief sketch will provide the correct context for a proper understanding of Paul and John, the two main witnesses, it is claimed, to trinitarian thinking in the New Testament.

Let us begin with Paul. There are repeated references to the Jewish *Shema* in his letters and in those written in his name: 1 Thess 1:9; Gal 3:20; Rom 3:30; 1 Cor 8:4,6; Eph 4:6. Equally Paul differentiates between the Christian belief about God from the prevailing paganism, borrowing repeatedly from Jewish invective against idolatry: 1 Thess 4:5; 1 Cor 8:5; 12:1-2; Gal 4:8-11. The Pauline missionary strategy was to give the communities that had formed around his preaching a sense of internal cohesion and strong boundaries, as well as a sense of unity with other Christian groups in the various cities of the eastern Mediterranean. To achieve this purpose he could draw freely on aspects of both Jewish and pagan talk about God, while at the same time insist on the distinctiveness of the Christian perspective as this had been definitively disclosed for Paul in the death and resurrection of Jesus.[8]

What differentiated Christians from Jews for Paul was not their understanding of God as one, but the issue of how belief in a crucified messiah as redeemer of a fallen human family could be integrated into their shared understanding of God, and the social implications of such a belief for Jews and gentiles. The symbol of the Spirit with both its Jewish and pagan associations was to play a vital role in this regard.[9] In common with the Greek world, Paul also thinks of *pneuma* itself as having a subtle corporeality, yet it stands over against the flesh (*sarx*) in representing the spiritual as distinct from the material aspect of reality. From the Jewish perspective God's spirit is a manifestation of God's power distinct from but active in the world renewing and restoring Israel. The resurrection of Jesus is for Paul the supreme manifestation of God's activity in the world, whereby he receives a spiritual body, itself a thoroughly Greek conception (1 Cor 15). Yet, as the Risen one, Jesus has become a life-giving spirit through this active power of God, sharing in God's transformative power for the world in line with the Jewish perception (Rom 8:2-6). He cannot then be equated with any of the *daimones* or lesser spiritual beings that peopled the heavens in the rather tolerant cosmic vision of Greco-Roman monotheism, even of the philosophical type. Yet the patterns of thought that had been fashioned by Philo and other hellenised Jews within that philosophical tradition provided the model for integrating belief in Jesus as Lord with the Jewish monotheistic declaration. In those circles as we have seen, the oneness and immateriality of God did not preclude thinking of the *logos*, or sensible representation as God also. Paul's own Jewish faith tipped the scales in favour of the Jewish monotheism as providing the basic framework, but a monotheism that nevertheless could co-opt the Greek tradition sufficiently to break with the more rigid thinking which the later rabbinic debates mirror. But it was with the Greek philosophical tradition that Paul identified rather than with that of pagan religiosity whose practices and beliefs the philosphers had sought to shed for some time. Thus Cynic-Stoic ethical ideals were naturally incorporated into the framework provided by the Jewish belief system without in any way endangering the distinctive understanding of God that that system entailed. It was a delicate balance, but a blend that clearly had a powerful social appeal, despite the initial struggles with Jews and subsequently with the pagan ethos also.[10]

The letters to the Corinthians and Romans give us some window on this complex process of community building and theological defining. Addressing the Jewish interlocutor in Romans, Paul asks: 'Is God the God of the Jews only?' To which the answer is: 'Yes, the God of the Gentiles also, since God is one' (3:29f). The implications of this are developed throughout the letter in terms of the universal human dilemma that has been made right by God in Christ. When Paul seeks to draw out those implications for the individual who has been baptised into Christ, in Rom 8, it is the Spirit that is at once the criterion and source of their participation in the new life. This spirit is described as the Spirit of God, the Spirit of Christ, Christ simply and the Spirit of him who raised Jesus from the dead – all in the space of a few short verses (Rom 8:9-11).

At Corinth, one issue is that of idolatry through the eating of meat sacrificed to idols. The strong dismiss the idea of polytheistic associations of such a practice, declaring that God is one, ironically rejecting the so-called gods in heaven and on earth of the pagan belief system. To this Paul replies with what appears to be a baptismal formula known to all: 'For us', he declares in a clear amplification of the traditional hellenistic-Jewish assertion that God is one, 'there is one God who is Father from whom are all things and for whom we exist, and one Lord, Jesus Christ, through whom are all things and through whom we exist' (1 Cor 8:6). The revision of the Deuteronomic formula consists in the reintroduction of the title *kyrios* and its application to Jesus in line with the early Christian confession (Phil 2:11) together with the naming of the one God as Father (possibly due to Jesus' mode of address, but also in line with the Greek tradition where *pater panton,* Father of All, was applied to the Supreme God as an epithet). God as origin and end of all is contrasted with Christ as instrument, thus combining philosphico-cosmological speculations about creation with historico-soteriological perspectives on redemption, it would seem. Later in the same epistle (1 Cor 12:4-6) when dealing with the divisions in the community because of the variety of charismata, the same formula is expanded further by inclusion of the Spirit. There are varieties of charisms, ministries and deeds, but one Spirit, one Lord, one God, whose role is described inclusively as 'the one who works all things in everyone' (*ho energon ta panta en pasin*). Here is no trinitarian model of perfect harmony to be imitated from afar, but a declaration of divine activity in the community, which is based on diverse gifts fittingly attributed to the Spirit, and diverse ministries equally aptly attributed to Christ, but with an underlying sense of unity that climaxes in the one God working all things in everyone.

This brief look at a few key Pauline passages where early Christian social experience and the naming of God coalesce shows great flexibility and dexterity with the various pre-texts available in the culture, Jewish and Greek, yet with a definite sense of boundaries provided by the Jewish belief system. The new life in Christ is the determining reality, or as E. Schillebeeckx says, the critical variant that determines both the social dimensions of early Christian existence and the co-relative naming of God. The expression of such beliefs through ritual, particularly in the rite of initiation, was obviously the place where these various ways of talking about God's activity was most likely to find a formalised expression. When however, these liturgical formulae were translated into Greek metaphysical language independently of their living context of worship, they lost their dynamic and active sense, and could all too easily become abstractions removed from the life of belief, worship and practice. That was never the intention of those who first named God in this way, least of all Paul, nor for that matter those who took the next step of expressing Christian faith in the philosophical categories of the day.

On entering the Johannine thought world, one receives a very different impression from that of Paul's less disciplined and unfinished thinking. The issues in debate in Jn 5 about the equality of Jesus with God would have been familiar to both a Greco-Roman and a Jewish readership, but with very different matters at stake. For the latter there is an echo here of later rabbinic speculation about the heretical implications of the 'two powers in heaven', already alluded to. For the Greco-Roman reader on the other hand the notion of equality with God did not have the same far-reaching implications. Isocrates, e.g. says: 'to be like God is to be a benefactor and to tell the truth'. In other words, the expression had strong ethical connotations. Good people can become friends of God and be called God. Yet it is clear that the Johannine Christians have to defend themselves against a far more serious charge. Jesus has made himself equal with God (5:18; or a God, 10:33, or God's son 19:7) and thus was guilty of blasphemy. These Christians had suffered persecution because of the claims which they made on Jesus' behalf and they had been expelled from the synagogue. Yet they held fast to the belief, not that Jesus had made himself God, but that he was God, by sharing in the powers to judge and to give life which he had received from the Father and which Scripture had reserved for God alone. Wayne Meeks has recently suggested that the Jewish mystical exegetical tradition, which laid special claim to insights into the secret meaning of Scripture, lay behind the Johannine Christians' claims, epitomised in the declaration: 'the one who has seen me has seen the Father' (14:9)[11] Such a conviction brought with it the social pain of expulsion, but also the compensation of a close-knit sense of intimacy, based on mutual love rather than the hierarchical ordering of community life. This was the truth that set them free, and which they audaciously sought to ground in their very special reading of the Jewish tradition.

The Johannine Christians could lay claim to the special gift of the Spirit in order to assist them in the daring enterprise of coming to a correct understanding of Jesus' life, an understanding that would set them apart socially and theologically from both the Jews and the world. In keeping with the two-stage notion of revelation as a remembering of Jesus in the post-resurrection period, the gift of the Spirit in the book of the signs is always associated with an understanding of the word that has been spoken.[12] In the farewell discourses this gift is named as the Paraclete who is identified with the Holy Spirit and the Spirit of Truth (Jn 14:17,26; 15:26; 16:13). Raymond Brown's discussion of these passages shows that the Paraclete functions solely in regard to Jesus, teaching and reminding the disciples about him, bearing witness to him, speaking only what he hears and expounding the things that are to come.[13] With such a brief, the Paraclete is at once totally subordinate and yet free to lead the community into the things that are to come, just as the Johannine Christ is totally subordinate to the Father and yet acts on his own initiative. The Paraclete functions like the interpreting angel of Jewish apocalyptic, disclosing the hidden mystery of God to the elect. And the Johannine Christians certainly consider themselves as the elect.

This brief reflection on the Johannine Christology and Pneumatology suggests that when these developments are put in their proper social, literary and theological settings, they are far removed from the abstract philosophical speculation that was to be the hallmark of later Trinitarian theology that had become divorced from the economy of salvation. These high points of early Christian God-talk are to be seen as another attempt by a sophisticated early Christian group to express their own social and religious experience in a highly distinctive manner. At the same time it bears the unmistakable marks of its setting at the cross-roads of Jewish and Greek speculations about God's presence and activity in the world.

Behind this theological development and provoking its on-going exploration stands the figure of the historical Jesus. The paradox of proclaiming precisely this figure as God was not lost on Celsus: 'They worship to an extravagant degree this man who appeared recently' (*Contra Celsum* VIII, 12). The Greek world was quite familiar with the notion of the gods manifesting themselves in human form as Paul and Barnabas had learned at Lystra (Acts 14:11-13; cf. Acts 28:6). Nevertheless, the anti-Christian polemic which Celsus represents sought to discredit Christian belief about Jesus by pointing to his lowly origins and his magical deceptions. His Jewish opponents had sought to discredit him also by attributing his exorcisms to witchcraft, whereas he himself had claimed that they pointed to the inbreaking of the kingly rule of God in his ministry to the destitute and the marginalised (Mk 3:22). By identifying the kingly rule of God in this way, rather than in cosmic upheavals, Jesus' proclamation posed a serious threat to the received notion of God that identified God's presence with the Jerusalem temple. The material blessings that were deemed to accrue to those who observed faithfully the stipulated worship were regarded as signs of that presence, despite the hierarchical and patriarchal ordering of life that was thereby legitimated.

The process of reflection that must have begun already during the public ministry as to the significance of Jesus' life became explicit in the light of the death/resurrection experience and quickly identified Jesus himself with the message he had proclaimed. This basic belief found varied expressions in the different communities of believers that soon emerged around the new movement, each drawing on its own cultural and religious antecedents in terms of hopes for definitive salvation – apocalyptic, wisdom, even gnostic. The proclaimer had become the proclaimed, in Bultmann's pithy phrase. In a variety of hymns and doxologies, mainly in the Greek-speaking churches, early Christian faith searched for ever more adequate expressions of its beliefs about Jesus,[14] culminating in the theologies of John and Paul which we have briefly discussed in this paper. It was inevitable that other philosophical categories would come into play as Christianity sought to establish its credentials as a *vera philosophia* not a *superstitio* in the Roman world. However, this necessary development should not have obscured the experiential and experimental nature of its own foundational texts by silencing their varied accents in one overarching system which increasingly veiled the human face of God as this had been encountered in the career of Jesus.

Notes

1. See B. Halpern, '"Brisker Pipes than Poetry": The Development of Israelite Monotheism', in J. Neusner et al. eds., *Judaic Perspectives on Ancient Israel* (Philadelphia: Fortress Press, 1987) 77-115, for a stimulating discussion of the emergence of a self-conscious monotheism in Israel through the axial period of its history (800-200 BCE) under political and social pressures.

2. For a brief but useful summary of these ideas, see H. Chadwick, *Origen, Contra Celsum* (Cambridge: CUP, 1953) xvi -xxii.

3. In the *Contra Apionem* (2, 165-167) Josephus writes:'Our law-giver (Moses) was attracted to none of these forms of government, but gave his constitution the form of what ... may be termed a theocracy. To him he persuaded all to look, as the author of all blessings, both those that were common to all mankind and those which they had won for themselves by prayer in the crises of their history. He represented him as one, uncreated and immutable to all eternity; in beauty surpassing all mortal thought, made known to us by his power, although the nature of his real being passes knowledge.'

4. J. Dillon, 'Logos and Trinity:Patterns of Platonist Influence in Early Christianity', in G. Vesey, ed., *The Philosophy in Christianity* (Cambridge: CUP, 1989) 1- 13.

5. See A. Chester, *Divine Revelation and Divine Titles in the Pentateuchal Targumim* (Tubingen: J.C.B. Mohr, 1986) especially, 293-324; B. Chilton, *The Isaiah Targum* (Edinburgh: T.&T. Clark, 1987) xvif.

6. See A. Segal, *Two Powers in Heaven. Early Rabbinic Reports about Christianity and Gnosticism* (Leiden: E.J. Brill, 1977) for a discussion of the relevant rabbinic texts and an attempt at identifying the heretics who were deemed to hold such unorthodox views. For a more general account of divine agency in the world in Jewish thought, see L. Hurtado, *One God, One Lord. Early Christian Devotion and Ancient Jewish Monotheism* (London: SCM, 1988).

7. As an example of how such ideas operated at the popular level, a second century CE inscription from Samaria is as follows: 'One God, Lord of all, Great maiden, the invincible.' Here instead of the usual consort deities the one god combines Kore/Persephone and Sol Invictus. For a discussion, see G. Horsley, *New Documents Illustrating Early Christianity*, Number One (Sydney: Macquarrie University, 1981) 105-107.

8. See N. Dahl, 'The One God of Jews and Gentiles', in *Studies in Paul* (Minneapolis: Augsburg, 1977) 178-191 for an excellent treatment of the issue of monotheism in Paul's thought.
9. See the article *pneuma* in *TDNT* (eds. G. Kittel and G. Friedrich) V1, 332-451, especially 357-59 and 424-36.
10. See W. Meeks, *The Moral World of the First Christians* (London: SPCK, 1986) especially 130-36; also A. Malherbe, *Paul among the Popular Philosophers* (Minneapolis: Fortress, 1990).
11. W. Meeks, 'Equal to God' in R. Fortna and B. Gaventa, eds., *The Conversation Continues. Studies in Paul and John in Honor of J.L. Martyn* (Nashville: Abingdon Press, 1990) 309-321.
12. See J. Ashton, *Understanding the Fourth Gospel* (Oxford: Clarendon Press, 1991).
13. R.E. Brown, *The Gospel According to John,* Anchor Bible vol. 29A (New York: Doubleday, 1970) Appendix V, The Paraclete, 1135-1144.
14. For a balanced and well documented account of this process see the several essays on early Christological reflection among the Hellenists in M. Hengel, *Between Jesus and Paul* (London: SCM, 1983) especially chapters one, two and five. Hurtado, *One God, One Lord,* 101-8 argues that public prayer to Christ in hymnic form was already a feature of Aramaic speaking, Jewish Christianity and as such introduces a further 'mutation' in the divine agency category within Judaism which he has outlined earlier in his study.

CHAPTER FOUR

The Nicene Heritage

Rowan Williams

The creed of Nicaea is a first step in the critical demythologising of Christian discourse. This may sound a wildly eccentric judgment: isn't the Nicene doctrine of the Trinity a capitulation to the most arrant mythological irresponsibility, binding the Church to an indefensible confidence about what is essentially hidden and unsayable, the life of God *as* God, independent of the world? Quite the opposite, I think. Pre-Nicene theologies of the Trinity had worked in two major ways, a cosmological mode and a liturgical mode. In the context of the former, trinitarian language functioned as part of a solution to the problem of how a transcendent God could establish contact with the world, or indeed *make* the world in the first place. In the context of the latter, the imagery of apocalyptic access to the heavenly sanctuary was used so as to position Christ and the Spirit as paradigm worshippers of the Father, or – in the case of Christ – High Priest of the heavenly temple, offering sacrifice and intercession for the world. In both, Christ – and, less securely, the Holy Spirit – can be said to function as a channel for divine meaning to be transmitted between creator and creation, whether by imparting to the world the rationality of God's mind or by providing the definition for the redeemed creature's eschatological standing before God.

The Arian crisis – or, more accurately, the bundle of inter-related doctrinal issues that became entangled with the name of Arius – put both modes in question; and the bitterness and complexity of the controversy had a lot to do with the manifest fact that the language of Nicaea and of its greatest defender, Athanasius, represented a breach with these two traditional idioms. The focal question was about the unity and the liberty of divine action: if God created and redeemed 'through' the Logos, the Son, was the act of making and saving God's own act or not? If not, if God were obliged to deal with creation only through a mediating reality, what did this say about God's freedom? Should we not be faced with the threatening possibility of an infinite regress of mediators? Arius's reply, careful and sophisticated, was that God simply chose to create one being, a Son or Word, capable of carrying or transmitting as much of the divine glory as possible to other creatures. But the Athanasian reply moved attention from what is *shown* in the Son to what is *done,* and insisted on pressing the issue of who is the agent of our making and remaking. If God alone is free enough for this, God alone acts in effecting it: what we must learn from revelation is that this act is 'articulated', a complex unity, an act that is eternally both an initiating and an answering.

Fourth century theology wrestles with how to say this without simply saying 'there are three divine agents': Cappadocian and Augustinian theology are diverse solutions to this (though not as diverse as they are sometimes thought to be). No-one wholly avoids anthropomorphism. But what Nicaea has excluded is a model of God 'first' existing in pure divine solitude or singleness, then deciding to create, then shaping instruments without which God cannot constitute or deal with contingent reality. Thus (i) God is not an individual with a psychology – i.e. a planning, problem-solving, reflective subject whose mental and other acts have a history; (ii) God's freedom is not a primal abyss of indeterminacy, subsequently 'focussed' by an act of naked or groundless will; (iii) transcendence is not distance but difference – i.e. not a problematic gap to be negotiated but the sheer fact of the difference between unconditioned act and acts that are set within a system of cause and chance. There is no *story* of God as Trinity, no mythical cosmogony (first the logos, then the world); the continuity of what Christ and the Spirit do with the agency that sustains the universe requires a model of God as irreducibly manifold act – as being concretely what God is eternally, necessarily and only in this manifoldness. It is not simply that a sequential and complex history of salvation is being directly projected onto the heavens, nor that speculative confidence has exceeded human limitations; it is rather the recognition that what Christians understand as divine agency has features that can only be made sense of if the divine life is agreed to be such as to make *that* kind of action (as seen in the history of creation, covenant, redemption) natural to it. An agency that appears in gift, response and the diffusion of the gift-response movement needs grounding in an appropriate set of rules for talking of its source. This is not to claim a conceptual grasp of what it's *like* to be God, only to try and guarantee that what's said of God allows for the full implications of how we encounter the freedom or creative resource that does not come from any pattern of circumstance in the universe, any set of finite causes.

It is not in tension with the apophatic. Properly speaking, it reinforces the apophatic impulse, in confronting us simultaneously with the narrative of Israel, Jesus and the Church, and with an austerely formal structure for referring to the God who gives coherence to the narrative, and of whom nothing can be said *substantively* but that this God is such as to give coherence to this narrative, that we meet this God thus and are constrained to organise what we say thus. At a time when it is fashionable to construct imaginative models of divine subjectivity, the interaction of more or less distinct divine consciousnesses (Brown, Moltmann), this austerity is important if we are actually to talk of a God who delivers us from the slavery of the world *by being free,* by being what God is, rather than being enmeshed in dramas of the psyche comparable to our own.

That Nicaea also paid a high price for this clarity cannot be denied. Plenty of later theologies of the Trinity, serving as tests for the professional skills of a professional class of theological ideolgues, as mystifications, focussed on the austerity while forgetting its ground in the way divine agency is historically met; and the erosion of earlier liturgical/apocalyptic imagery led to a weakening of a proper theology of Christ's *human* priesthood, and of a lively sense of the worshipping Christ, *verus Deus, verus homo,* as defining our vocation (a theme repeatedly and fruitfully explored in T.F. Torrance's work on this subject). But this issue is not resolved by denying distinctions between immanent and economic Trinity, or elevating the latter over the former; it requires us to sustain the tension between a human history and a grammatical scheme. And so to sustain this is the task of participating in what the divine agency effects in us, not least in the gift of that contemplative silence which is where Christ's action and passion leads us, and in the work of communicating human communion, liberty and dignity, the work we identify as what the Spirit does. In short, sustaining the tension is part of what Bonhoeffer simply called 'prayer and just action'. Nicaea, I believe, should bring us to this point, not to a revived world of cosmogonic fantasy, nor to a self-justifying conceptual minuet. It tells Christian theology that between what is seen in history and what is seen in silence, there is no gap to insert speculative dramas for heavenly individuals, because in the incarnate Word the history and the unsayable resource of divine act are no longer to be pulled apart.

CHAPTER FIVE

The Triune God of Grace:

The Doctrine of the Trinity in the Theology of the Reformers

Christoph Schwöbel

When one considers the significance of the theology of the Reformers on the way towards exploring the possibilities of a contemporary trinitarian theology, one feels tempted to refer to the allegedly Irish wisdom offered in response to the disoriented traveller asking for directions: 'If I were going there, I wouldn't start from here.' The standard textbooks on the theology of the Reformers create the impression that the Trinity is certainly not one of their major concerns. Paul Althaus' *The Theology of Martin Luther,* in most other respects a rather full account of Luther's thought, treats Luther's teaching on the Trinity on two pages.[1] He states that Luther affirmed the orthodox doctrine of the Trinity because he sees it stated in Scripture, both in the Old and in the New Testament. He emphasizes that Luther spent considerable effort on discussing the doctrine in academic disputations and expounding its implications and applications in sermons. However, according to Althaus it has to be observed that Luther maintained a critical distance from the 'subtleties' of the scholastics and rejected any attempts to deduce the Trinity from the divine essence in order to make it accessible to human reason.[2] Faith based on the witness of Scripture is the access to the doctrine of the Trinity, natural reason leads to heresy and error. In all other respects, Althaus states, Luther follows Augustine in his trinitarian teaching.[3] When we turn to Werner Elert's treatment in *Morphologie des Luthertums,* an account otherwise not known for extreme economy of exposition, we find an even more condensed statement on one page.[4] He states that Luther affirms the unity of the divine essence and the unity of God in relation to creatures while affirming at the same time the threefold personal revelation of God. Furthermore, he points to the fact that Luther does not reduce the Trinity to 'a mere Trinity of revelation'. Rather, Luther retains the doctrine of the immanent relations of God's trinitarian being.

Elert, however, states that Luther does not attempt to explore it from his specific understanding of faith. In this way, Elert can say that 'in general' the doctrine of the Trinity remains in Luther's theology something like an 'erratic block'. In contrast to these rather bold statements, Elert mentions that the awareness of the significance of the doctrine of the Trinity was for Luther not a result of his opposition to the enthusiasts and their unitarian tendencies. In this context he mentions that as early as 1520 Luther calls the doctrine of the Trinity 'the highest article of faith in which all others hang',[5] but he interprets that as an expression of the central place of belief in Christ for Luther's theology. On the whole, both authors give a somewhat uninformative account that could hardly persuade us to start from here on our way towards a contemporary trinitarian theology.

With regard to Calvin the situation seems a little better, but not significantly different. One would expect that we would find in the standard textbooks a clear indication of the significance of the doctrine for the Genevan Reformation and its theologian since it forms the background of the only burning at the stake of a 'heretic' in the Reformation. However, even here the first impression seems disappointing, since commentators on Calvin's *Defensio orthodoxae fidei de sacra trinitate* against Michael Servetus emphasise that Calvin is not so much concerned with securing the orthodox doctrine of the Trinity, but with refuting Servet's Christology and its soteriological presuppositions and implications.[6] In this sense we find that a standard textbook like Wilhelm Niesel's *Theology of Calvin* emphasises that the purpose of Calvin's doctrine of the Trinity is to protect the biblical message that God is revealed in the flesh against misunderstanding.[7] This could claim support from the *Institutes* where the scriptural evidence for the divinity of the Son of God is indeed one of the main foci of the exposition.[8] However, if securing the divinity of the mediator is the predominant purpose of Calvin's doctrine of the Trinity, it seems remarkable that he spent considerable technical expertise on the effort to clarify his trinitarian thinking. Calvin distinguishes, for instance, the *subsistentia* of the three persons in the one divine essence by indicating the *proprietas* of Father, Son and Spirit which as their personal particularity is incommunicable. Furthermore, we find that for Calvin there is in the divine Trinity a certain order, *dispositio vel oeconomica,* which does not impair the unity of the divine essence, but nevertheless offers clear distinctions of the trinitarian persons through the inner-trinitarian relations. In all this Calvin seems to depart from a standard reading of Augustine's theology of the Trinity and takes up important insights of the trinitarian logic developed by the Cappadocians.[9] This seems especially apparent in Calvin's trinitarian account of divine action where he attributes to the Father the beginning of all effects, the fount and origin of all things, the Son as the wisdom, the counsel and the distribution of all divine works and the Holy Spirit as the power and efficacy in all divine actions. (*Patri principium agendi, rerumque omnium fons et scaturigo attribuitur: Filio sapientia, consilium, ipsaque in rebus agendis dispensatio: at Spiritui virtus et efficacia assignatur actionis.*[10]) However, if we follow Niesel all this is intended to secure the unity of God who is in this way distinguished from idols and is proclaimed as the Lord whom we encounter in revelation.[11] All we seem to gain from these standard descriptions of the doctrine of the Trinity in the reformers is that the reformers were perfectly orthodox in their affirmation of the doctrine of the Trinity, but that the Trinity remained somehow without decisive implications for their theology, apart from supporting their christological doctrines. The question I want to raise is whether this account is correct as it stands. Could it be that the authors' own preoccupation with christological matters and their somewhat underdeveloped view of the creative possibilities of trinitarian theology prevented them from seeing the full significance of the Trinity for the reformers? Is it perhaps misleading to look for a fully-fledged theoretical development of the traditional doctrine of the Trinity in the reformers? Should we not rather try to find out whether they developed a trinitarian theology which was necessary to support their main contentions for the reconstruction of theology and the reformation of the church?

In the following I will attempt to indicate five points which seem to me crucial for assessing the significance of the Trinity for the theology of the reformers, for finding out whether the reformers' thought represents a significant stage on the way towards the development of a contemporary trinitarian theology.

1. The first point that determines the distinctive perspective of

Reformation theology is that it interprets the doctrine of grace as the organising centre of all theological thought. That is generally and, more specifically, ecumenically, agreed. It was Karl Rahner who emphasized that medieval theology had not developed a unified and comprehensive doctrine of grace. This could only be done, Rahner states, after Reformation theology had brought the enterprise of theology as a whole under the perspective of justification.[12] The continuity and discontinuity of Reformation theology with the preceding and subsequent theological tradition becomes clear from this perspective. It explains to what extent the reformers took up the traditional teachings on grace, especially from the Augustinian tradition, and attempted a comprehensive reconstruction of the doctrine of grace, a reconstruction which, however, was at the same time an effective deconstruction of the late medieval penitential system.

In many ways the reformers' understanding of grace is based on a retrieval of the original radicalism of Augustine's doctrine of sin and grace. In the form it finds in his late writings after 425 Augustine's teaching on grace is focused on two points: his view of original sin and his understanding of the efficacy of divine grace which leads to his doctrine of predestination. Original sin is the state which is brought about by the abuse of the *liberum arbitrium* by the first human and is characterized by the loss of the *adiutorium gratiae* providing orientation for the human will and therefore by the bondage of the will in sin.[13] The efficacy of God's grace in Christ which is administered in the word and the sacraments brings about the justification of the sinner, the liberation from original sin and is the cause for the perseverance of faith. As such it does not restore free will, but in effect replaces it and is therefore irresistible.[14] This implies that the foundation of God's grace in vocation, justification and the perserverance of faith cannot be seen in human merit, but only in God's predestination.[15] There is a certain ambiguity about the legacy of Augustinianism in the church. From the Synod of Orange (529) on this radical conception was partially approved and partially rejected by the church. What is approved is the understanding of original sin as the radical inability of fallen human nature to will and to do the good unaided, the emphasis on the necessity of grace for willing the good and the stress on the continuing dependence on divine grace after justifying grace has been received. What is not approved or is even explicitly rejected is Augustine's emphasis on the irretrievable loss of free will, the view of the irresistibility of grace and his view of the predestination excluding, as it were, the salvific significance of human merit. The partial approval and partial rejection of Augustine's radical interpretation of sin and grace contains the explosive constellation of questions which fuelled the long drawn out medieval debates between Dominican and Franciscan theologians on freedom and grace.[16]

Over against this constellation of problems and their attempted solutions Luther re-asserts the radicalism of Augustine's position and even takes this radicalism one step further by approaching the question of grace from the perspective of the distinction between divine work and human work, famously developed in the debate with Erasmus as the distinction between *virtus Dei et nostra* and *opus Dei et nostrum*.[17] This includes the reaffirmation of the total inability of human nature to do the good, and thereby to contribute to a human disposition for receiving divine grace, and the understanding of the efficacy of grace as the total transformation of the human heart, of the affective life of the human person.[18] Luther emphasises with increasing clarity that the change of the 'habits of the heart' is itself based on the disclosure by the Spirit of the truth of the Gospel of Christ which is proclaimed in preaching and by the 'visible words' of the sacraments. This is the passively constituted insight into the believer's relationship to God as that of a justified sinner to the justifying God.[19] This determines the total perspective of Christian theology as *cognitio Dei et hominis*.[20]

2. The second point is that the distinctive re-ordering of the doctrine of grace which the reformers attempted has its focus in interpreting the event of divine grace as the representation of the revelation of Christ in the Spirit.[21] God's grace becomes effective in the disclosure experience which reveals and discloses the Gospel of Christ to the believer and thus incorporates the believer into the actualisation of God's will for his creation. Revelation is no longer seen as the supernaturally disclosed true account of revelatory events which is given as the subject-matter of faith in the medium of authoritative tradition. Revelation is interpreted as the work of God the Holy Spirit who discloses for the elect the truth of the Gospel of Christ in such a way that it enables them to have faith as unconditional trust in God and unconditional obed-

ience to his commandments. The gift of grace is the free and sovereign work of the Holy Spirit in authenticating the external word of Scripture. The reformers' preference for personal discourse about God the Spirit over against the causal interpretation of the language of grace and, together with this, especially in Calvin, their recovery of the pre-Augustinian terminology of Spirit-discourse, is intended to press home the one point that grace is God's free gift which can neither be effectively administered by a holy institution nor incorporated in human acts.[22] Rather, it is God the Spirit who incorporates and instrumentalises the human acts of witnessing to the truth of the Gospel in his action and thus creates the possibility of faith in the first place. This leads to a radical restructuring of the doctrine of the Holy Spirit which can be most clearly seen in Luther's reorganisation of the catechetical instruction for Christian believers.[23] Luther reduces the twelve articles of the Apostles' Creed to three using the trinitarian framework for Christian faith as the ordering principle. In the (now) third article 'I believe in the Holy Spirit' he subsumes all the subsequent beliefs, the church, that is, the communion of saints, the forgiveness of sins and the resurrection of the flesh and eternal life under the heading of the activity of the Holy Spirit. Far from being independent *credenda* they are seen as the means and ways in which the Spirit exercises his work. Although Luther retains the concept of sanctification to characterise the Spirit's work, this process now covers not only a partial and preliminary stage in the drama of salvation. It comprises the whole dynamic of God's trinitarian action.[24] In the Spirit's work the activity of the Father in creation and the work of the Son in reconciliation are actualised, made present and directed towards their future perfection.

3. With this we have arrived at the third point which seems of significance for assessing the reformers' thought on the Trinity. It is their reshaping of the doctrine of grace in terms of the free activity of God the Spirit which leads to a new emphasis on God's trinitarian action.[25] The reinterpretation of Spirit discourse makes it necessary that the activity of God the Spirit is seen as the perfection and actualisation of the work of the Father and the Son. In this sense one can say that for Luther in the Apostles' Creed the stress of the first and second articles is on the work of the Father and of the Son, whereas the third article states how this work is

perfected. Luther can even describe this as the defining characteristic of the Spirit: He is the one in whom the Father, through and with the Son, effects everything and brings everything to life.[26] The work of the Spirit is therefore the form of God's trinitarian action.[27] We can distinguish the material characteristics of the work of the Father, creation, and the work of the Son, redemption, but these material aspects have their unity in the work of the Spirit. The mode in which the Spirit represents God's trinitarian action to us is described by Luther as one of co-presence. The Spirit makes us co-present with God's acts in the past and in the future in memory and hope.[28] We are thereby located in the horizon of the totality of God's activity as the creator of everything there is, as the redeemer of his alienated creation and as the one who brings us to the sanctified perfection of eternal life. The Spirit makes us co-present to God, and that is described as bringing us to Christ and through Christ to the Father by being God's trinitarian co-presence for us. The point of this trinitarian account of divine action is that it is described as a threefold divine self-giving. Luther says in the conclusion of the pneumatological article in the *Greater Catechism* that in the Creed 'we perceive how God has given Himself to us entirely, bestowing all He has upon us, to help and guide us in keeping the Ten Commandments: The Father gives us all things created, Christ all His works, and the Holy Spirit all His gifts.'[29] It is in this pneumatological perspective that God's trinitarian action is represented as a threefold divine self-giving: '... besides having bestowed on us all that is in heaven and on earth, He gave us also His Son and the Holy Spirit, through whom He brings us to Himself. For (...) we could never recognise the Father's grace and mercy except for our Lord Christ, who is a mirror of his Father's heart; without Him we should see nothing but an angry and terrible Judge, and of Christ we should know nothing were He not revealed to us through the Holy Spirit.'[30] The upshot of this has been concisely summarised by Eilert Herms: the economic Trinity is the *self*-manifestation of the immanent Trinity.[31]

4. This account of God's trinitarian work – and this is the fourth point – does not remain external to the life of the believer. In the reformers' view it is constitutive for the life of faith because in the threefold divine self-giving God gives believers their own life as that of reconciled and sanctified creatures. 'For He created us in

order that He might redeem and sanctify us.'[32] It is against the background of this understanding of the trinitarian work of God that Calvin's thesis of the mutual dependence of self-knowledge and the knowledge of God receives its deepest confirmation. It is in knowing God the Father, the Son and the Spirit, in the self-manifestation of God as sanctifier, redeemer and creator, that human beings are enabled to understand their own life as created, redeemed and called into the process of sanctification which finds its fulfilment in the eternal life. And it is in experiencing their own life in faith as that of sanctified and redeemed creatures that they gain access to an ever deeper understanding of the triune God who is the creator, redeemer and sanctifier of his creation. With this interpretation of human existence in the light of God's trinitarian action the reformers liberate the doctrine of the Trinity from its ivory tower in the pious speculation of the intricacies of the doctrine of the immanent Trinity and from its relegation to a sacred sphere of worship separated from the ordinary exercise of the life of faith. If Christian faith is in its very nature reflective faith and if the whole life of faith in all its aspects is a life of worship, then all reflection of faith is trinitarian theology and all praxis of faith is esssentially trinitarian.

5. My last point can be very brief: What the reformers attempted, and I would claim, succeeded in doing, was not a reformulation of the *doctrine* of the Trinity. It was an application of the doctrine of Trinity to all spheres of theology so that they could be seen as aspects of trinitarian theology. This they achieved by giving Christian theology a decisive soteriological orientation which, in turn, was based on a reformulated understanding of the work of God the Spirit. From this foundation they could develop a trinitarian view of divine action which interpreted the work of the Trinity as a three-fold divine self-giving, so that the economic Trinity could be seen as the self-manifestation of the immanent Trinity. This heritage is not without creative ambiguities and critical problems: Hegel as well as Karl Barth can only be understood on this foundation. It would, however, seem that the *applied trinitarian theology* of the reformers has still something to offer for contemporary theological reflection.

One could point to two aspects of the contemporary theological situation which can illustrate the continuing relevance of the reformers' trinitarian theology. The first concerns the relationship between the Eastern and the Western theological traditions in contemporary reflections on the Trinity. The renaissance of trinitarian theology in the last fifteen years has received many creative impulses from the exchange between Eastern orthodox trinitarian theology and Western theological traditions. The understanding of the triune God as Persons in Communion has helped Western theology a great deal to conduct a critical reappraisal of its non-trinitarian 'theistic' heritage and to break the link between a unitarian conception of God and a purely individualistic understanding of persons – divine and human.[33] Yet there is also a danger here that this new trinitarian emphasis will simply displace the preoccupation of the Western theological tradition with the question of grace in which no lesser theologian than Luther saw the essence of Christianity. The reformers have pointed to the mutual interdependence of the understanding of grace and the understanding of the triune God in God's trinitarian action which is based on their view that the gracious justification of the sinner *is* the way in which the trinitarian divine economy is actualised. This insight merits further exploration if we do not want simply to exchange the weaknesses of one tradition for those of another in the debate between Eastern and Western theologies.[34]

The second point is a more general *practical* theological illustration of the relevance of the reformers' trinitarian theology. One can argue that the most important ecumenical issue we encounter in the Church today is not the relationship *between* the different churches and denominations, but concerns the relationship between three groups which we find *within* most churches and denominations. It is, I think, no exaggeration to say that most ecclesial communities find themselves internally divided in three parts. There is, first of all, a group which strongly emphasises the fatherhood or motherhood of God in the context of a creation-centred spirituality and theology. The relationship between God and the world is understood in terms of a universal dependence on the divine source of creativity and the providential flourishing of creation. This group may consist of many, even conflicting groups, but it is the creation-centred emphasis which provides the basis even for their disagreements. Secondly, there is a group of Christians, often calling themselves 'evangelicals', whose spirituality and theology is strongly, if not exclusively, focused on atonement and redemption. With this focus is often combined an emphasis on human sin and fallenness and on an understanding of God which sees the redeemer Jesus without much qualification as God. In extreme forms this may come close to a 'unitarianism of the Second Person'. The third group, the charismatics, practise forms of worship with a heavy emphasis on the present power of the Spirit, reviving the rich metaphors of impersonal forces for the presence and activity of God, even in their self-interpretation as 'third wave' charismatics. It seems to me that the real ecumenical problem we face today is how these three groups can continue to live together in one ecclesial community, given that all three groups find it easy to associate with other groups representing their style of worship and theology in other churches. Here the reformers' insistence on the internal interconnectedness of God's trinitarian action which shapes the specifically Christian praxis of faith and which reflects the relational life of the triune God can help not only to identify the problem, but perhaps also to inspire attempts to seek for possible solutions.

If I were going there, I would not start from here ... Does our brief survey confirm our fictional advice to the traveller on the road towards an exploration of the theological possibilities opened up by the doctrine of the Trinity? Perhaps we can answer that if we were going there (and I hope we are) we should perhaps not start from here. Even the reformers did not; they started from the witness of Scripture and the orthdox doctrine of the Trinity they had received from the Fathers of the church. All I wanted to show is that we should not circumvent the reformers' applied trinitarian theology as an important stage, and perhaps a turning-point, on our path towards a fuller exploration of the doctrine of the Trinity. Nothing has been said implying that we should stop here.

Notes

1. cf. Paul Althaus, *Die Theologie Martin Luthers* (Gütersloh [5]1980) 175ff.
2. Althaus refers to WA 10 I, 181,11; 185,3; 193,6.9 where the 'subtleties' of the schoolmen are contrasted to the 'simple, awesome and clear words of scripture'.
3. The references which Althaus cites show, however, a more

qualified use of Augustine where the criterion for assenting to the trinitarian teaching of the patristic and scholastic theologians is again seen in Scripture. Cf. WA 39 II, 305,9: *'Ita tres personae et unus Deus in scriptura clarissime probantur. Neque enim crederem vel Augustini vel Magistri scriptis, nisi hunc de trinitate articulum vetus et novum testamentum liquidissime ostenderent.'* (cf. loc.cit. 175)

4. Werner Elert, *Morphologie des Luthertums, Bd. 1: Theologie und Weltanschauung des Luthertums* (Munich[3]: 1965) 190f.

5. '...höchst artikell ym glauben darynnen die andern alle hangen...' WA 7, 214, 27.

6. cf. Ernst Wolf, *'Deus omniformis.* Bemerkungen zur Christologie des Michael Servet,' *Theologische Aufsätze.* Karl Barth zum 50 Geburtstag (Munich: 1936) 450.

7. cf. Wilhelm Niesel, *Die Theologie Calvins* (Munich, 1938) 53.

8. *Inst* I, 13, 7-13.

9. This is emphasised in the modern literature by James P. Mackey, *The Christian Experience of God as Trinity* (London: 1983) 191: 'As far as concerns his own selective emphasis within inherited material, Calvin reminds one sometimes more of Gregory of Nyssa (and sometimes more of Philo) than of Augustine.' He adds the critical comment which highlights some of the conceptual problems in Calvin's account: 'If one coupled together, as one could also do with Gregory of Nyssa, those texts in which Calvin ... insists upon the utter incomprehensibility of the divine essence, his concomitant insistence that it is the work, power, or activity of God (God's *energeia*?) and not God's essence that is revealed, with his firm proposal that it is the *hypostasis* of the Father that is made known by the Son, one would have to wonder once again what is the relationship of the divine essence to the divine *hypostaseis* or 'persons'. One realises that none of these theologians wishes to arrive at a quaternity, and one hesitates to count Calvin, or even Gregory, amongst those theologians who seemed to place the Trinity itself on a level of the divine Being.' (191f.)

10. *Inst* I 13, 18. This recalls Basil's distinction in *De Spir.* XV, 38 between the Father as the originating cause of everything there is, the Son as the creative cause and the Spirit as the perfecting cause.

11. op.cit. 56.

12. cf. Karl Rahner, Art. Gnadentheologie, LThK [2]IV, 1010-1014, especially 1011.

13. cf. *De corr. et grat.* 12, 33-37.

14. cf. *De grat et lib. arb.* 5, 10-6, 13 and 17, 33.
15. cf. *De praed. sanct.* 2, 5-9; for the relationship between predestination and grace see especially 10, 19.
16. For the development of Augustine's view and its ambiguous history of reception see Ekkehard Mühlenberg 'Dogma und Lehre im Abendland' in: *Handbuch der Dogmen- und Theologiegeschichte, vol I: Die Lehrentwicklung im Rahmen der Katholizität* (Göttingen: 1982) 445-476.
17. WA 18, 614: *'Oportet igitur certissimam distinctionem habere inter virtutem Dei et nostram, inter opus Dei et nostrum, si volumus pie vivere.'* On the relationship between Augustine's and Luther's teaching on grace cf. Eilert Herms 'Gnade', in: *Offenbarung und Glaube. Zur Bildung des christlichen Lebens* (Tübingen: 1992) 1-19. cf. also O.H.Pesch and A.Peters, *Einführung in die Lehre von Gnade und Rechtfertigung* (Darmstadt: 1981).
18. Classically in the disputation *'Contra scholasticam theologiam'*, WA1, 224-228. For Calvin's view of the bondage of the will as implied in the total perversion of fallen human nature, cf. *Inst* II, 2-5 and II, 7-9. On the human heart as the affective centre of the human person which motivates and directs the choice of goals of action by the will, see especially *Inst* II, 4, 6.
19. cf. WA 40 II, 327f.
20. cf. Gerhard Ebelings' classic study 'Cognitio Dei et hominis', in: *Lutherstudien* Vol. I, (Tübingen: 1971) 221-272. The *locus classicus* of Calvin's treatment of the formula is, of course, *Inst* I,1,2. cf. E.A.Dowey, *The Knowledge of God in Calvin's Theology* (New York: 1965).
21. cf. for Luther's theology of the Spirit, Regin Prenter, *Spiritus Creator. Studien zu Luthers Theologie* (Munich: 1950); for Calvin cf. Werner Krusche, *Das Wirken des Heiligen Geistes nach Calvin* (Göttingen: 1957).
22. cf. for a systematic exploration of the changes the reformers introduced to pneumatology, Robert Jenson's treatment of the *locus* 'The Spirit', in: Carl E.Braaten Robert W. Jenson, eds., *Christian Dogmatics* (Philadelphia: 1984) vol. II, 105-178, especially 125-142. Calvin retains the whole field of concepts and metaphors of 'force' associated with the Spirit (e.g. *virtus, vigor, vis, potentia, energia, effectus, impulsus, motus, influxus* etc.), but interprets them as the 'force' of the 'person' of the Spirit which is a real *subsistentia in Dei essentia: 'Personam igitur voco subsistentiam in Dei essentia, quae*

ad alios relata, proprietate incommunicabili distinguitur.' Inst I 13, 6.
23. Eilert Herms has convincingly shown that the theology of the Spirit is in Luther's theology the summary account of Christian doctrine which discloses the unity of the confession of faith in the exposition of the relationship of faith in Father, Son and Spirit. This is not to be contrasted to the christological emphasis of Luther's exposition of the Creed, but demonstrates in which way the Christ event becomes constitutive for Christian faith. In developing this thesis Herms gives a concise account of Luther's trinitarian theology. cf. E. Herms, *Luthers Auslegung des Dritten Artikels* (Tübingen: 1987); for the main thesis see VIf.
24. The exposition of the process of sanctification is therefore an account of the content and process of revelation. cf. the detailed analysis in Herms, loc.cit. 65-99.
25. In his article 'Verborgener Gott – dreieiniger Gott nach Martin Luther' (in: Karl Rahner, ed., *Der eine und der dreieine Gott. Das Gottesverständnis bei Christen, Juden und Muslimen* (Zürich: 1983) 117-140) Albrecht Peters has observed an interesting parallelism between Luther's understanding of the hiddenness of God and his understanding of the doctrine of the Trinity. The notion of the *deus absconditus* is at first interpreted along the lines of Dionysius the Areopagite and Nicolaus of Cusa as an expression of the divine incomprehensibility. The *Dicata super Psalterium* of 1513-1515 speak of *Deus absconditus et incomprehensibilis* by explicitly referring to Pseudo-Denys and his mystical method of negation in ascending to the divine reality. WA 3,124,32: *'Dionysius docet ingredi in tenebras analogicas et per negationes ascendere. Quia sic est deus absconditus et incomprehensibilis.'* From 1518 onwards the hiddenness of God is explored in the context of Luther's *theologia crucis:* it is in the cross of Christ that we see *Deus crucifixus et absconditus.* For this formula cf. WA 1, 613,23; 614,19. From that time the *locus* of the hiddenness of God is the tribulations of faith in the world. Peters points to a similar development in Luther's understanding of the Trinity. Whereas early sources give evidence of traces of the speculative tradition of reflection on the immanent Trinity, we find from 1520 onwards a decisive turn to the explication of the Trinity in the context of the divine economy of grace. According to Peters it is the emphasis on divine revelation as it is witnessed in Scripture which leads Luther to abandon Augustine's explication of the immanent Trinity in terms of in-

ternally related mental acts of the human spirit and to turn to a stronger emphasis on the particularity of the trinitarian persons reminscent of the Victorines. (cf. loc.cit. 126ff.) The emphasis on the divine economy as occurring through the *word* of grace addressed to humanity through Christ and in the Spirit leads to an interesting inversion of trinitarian logic. Since the word of grace is addressed to humanity through the Son and in the Spirit, Luther postulates this structure of address as the form of the immanent trinitarian relationships. There is in the divine Trinity a 'pulpit' ('Predigstuhl') where God the Father utters his address in the Son and the Spirit listens to disclose this address to humanity. 'Gleich wie der Vater ein ewiger Sprecher ist, der Sohn in Ewigkeit gesprochen wird, ist also der Heilige Geist von Ewigkeit der Zuhörer' (WA 46, 60,4 cited in Peters 127). cf. also WA 28,51,20-53,24. cf. Reiner Jansen, *Studien zu Luthers Trinitätslehre* (Bern-Frankfurt: 1976).

26. cf. WA7, 218, 31.

27. W. Krusche expresses this in his interpretation of Calvin with admirable precision: 'Gott ist in der Seinsweise des Heiligen Geistes der sein Handeln im Sohn an dem von ihm geschaffenen Gegenüber zur Wirkung bringende, oder abgekürzt Gott ist heiliger Geist als der Wirksam Handelnde und der handelnd zur Wirkung Gelangende. Galt für die *immanente* Trinität die paradoxe Aussage, daß der Heilige Geist gerade durch sein vom *gignere* des Vaters und *gigni* des Sohnes unterschiedenes *procedere* der Vater und Sohn Verbindende ist, so gilt nun für das *trinitarische Wirken Gottes nach außen* ebenso paradox: das das Wirken des Geistes von dem des Vaters ind des Sohnes eigentümlich Unterscheidende ist dies, daß es gerade das Wirken des Vaters und des Sohnes zum Ziel bringt. Die eigentümliche Tat des Geistes ist gerade die, daß er nichts Eigenes tut, sondern das Tun des *Vaters* und des *Sohnes* verwirklicht. Alles, was Gott wirkt – und er wirkt alles und wirkt immer! – ist in seiner *Wirkung* Wirken des Heiligen Geistes. Es gibt schlechterdings kein Handeln des Vaters und des Sohnes, das wirksam würde ohne das Wirken des Geistes. Alles göttliche Handeln ist in seiner Spitze pneumatisch. Der Geist ist die *Dei manus, qua suam potentiam exercet.*' (loc.cit. 11) The concluding quotation from *Inst* III 1,3 shows Calvin's preference for this Irenaean metaphor for God's trinitarian action.

28. A recent attempt to explore the notion of 'co-presence' as the

key to the understanding of 'knowledge in the Spirit' has been undertaken by Ingolf U. Dalferth in his book *Kombinatorische Theologie. Probleme theologischer Rationalität* (Freiburg-Basel-Wien: 1991) chapter 3: 'Das Erkenntnisproblem: Heiliger Geist und menschliche Erkenntnis', 99-158, especially 144ff.

29. *Luther's Primary Works together with his Shorter and Larger Catechisms.* Translated into English, edited with theological and historical essays by H.Wace and C.A.Buchheim (London: 1896) 107.

30. op. cit. 106. Compare the conclusion of the exposition of the first article of the Creed: 'For here we may see how the Father has given Himself to us, with all He has created, and how abundantly He has cared for us in this life, besides which He has also overwhelmed us with unspeakable, everlasting blessings through His Son and the the Holy Spirit' (98). This emphasis on divine self-giving is continued in the opening of the exposition of the second article: 'Here we learn to know the Second Person of the Godhead, and we see what we have received from God besides the temporal goods already spoken of, namely, how He has poured out His whole self upon us, and kept back nothing, having bestowed everything upon us.' (99)

31. Herms, op. cit. 118: '...die ökonomische Trinität ist die Selbstmanifestation der immanenten.' Herms immediately adds in a footnote that this does not assert the simple identity of the immanent and the economic Trinity: 'Mit dieser Feststellung ist gerade nicht die immanente Trinität ihres Unterschieds gegenüber der ökonomischen beraubt. Es ist nur festgehalten, daß sie ausschließlich als Implikat der ökonomischen für uns Gegenstand (uns gegenwärtig) ist.' (*Ibid.* note 6)

32. *Greater Catechism*, loc. cit. 106.

33. cf. for instance John D. Zizioulas, *Being as Communion. Studies in Personhood and the Church* (London: 1985). The inspiration of a trinitarian theology based on the Cappadocians has been most creatively applied to central issues of the Western theological and intellectual tradition by Colin E.Gunton, *The Promise of Trinitarian Theology* (Edinburgh: 1991).

34. What is needed can almost be described as a mutual dialogical cross-fertilisation of a theological approach like that of J.D.Zizioulas in his 'On Being a Person. Towards an Ontology of Personhood' (in: Chr.Schwöbel/C.E.Gunton, eds., *Persons – Divine*

and Human (Edinburgh: 1991) 33-46) with the theological perspective presented by Wilfried Joest in his *Ontologie der Person bei Luther* (Göttingen: 1967).

PART II

Philosophical and Systematic Reflections on the Christian Understanding of God

CHAPTER SIX

Are there Christian Alternatives to Trinitarian Thinking?*

James P. Mackey

The most prominent feature of contemporary trinitarian theology has been the re-emergence of so-called social models of the Trinity, due mainly to the work of Jürgen Moltmann. These have been subject to persistent suspicion, sometimes expressed quite mildly as the suspicion that they do not sufficiently protect the unity of the divine being, sometimes as brashly and openly as in charges of tritheism. But they continue to recommend themselves, and to be defended, on the grounds of their alleged influence for creative improvement upon the structures of society in churches and states; they nourish more humane social relationships, it is said, than the more metaphysical doctrines of the Trinity in which, traditionally, the threeness was abstruse in formulation and, hence, quite submerged in more dominant impressions of a monotheistic, monarchial unity of the divine being.

When I first read Moltmann's *The Trinity and The Kingdom of God* I was impressed by his critique of the abstruseness and consequent practical irrelevance of traditional trinitarian theologies, and I felt that, in the absence of anything else, his social model might do some of the good he expected it to do. I have since become convinced that the introduction of the social model has resulted in a very great deal of damage indeed, done not only to trinitarian theology, but to the whole task of seeking a relevant Christian theology; and that the trinitarian theology of Augustine, for instance, did at least have the advantage of running out of meaning just at the point where we ought to be apophatic, that is to say, in attempting to describe the immanent structures of the divine being. For it is not the need for a social model as such that does the damage – the relationships between God, Jesus and those who make up the body of the church in the world provide a model as social as the most ardent socialist could desire; and the damage that is done is not exhaustively invoked by those who press the charge of tritheism – for, unless it happens to be false, as Christian monotheists think it is, there is probably nothing intrinsically unacceptable about belief in a happy, productive and harmonious Trinity of divine persons in the heavens. What is wrong, and can be very wrong in practical implications as well as in itself, is the projection of current ideas of human relationships into the divine being, resulting in an 'immanent' Trinity which then, of course, becomes normative (and not merely inspiring) for the reconstruction of human relationships in civic and ecclesiastical societies. This process turns our present perception of 'good relationships' into absolutes, and that is not a good thing even for our present perception of the good 'Christian' relationships, that is, those we believe that Jesus as Risen Lord still tries to foster in our midst, for of such processes ideologies are made.

But do the more recent trinitarian theologians construct an immanent Trinity in addition to the trinitarian structure of this divine 'economy'? Have they not rather moved beyond the addition of extra referents and do they not all now accept with enthusiasm Rahner's axiom: 'the immanent Trinity *is* the economic Trinity, and the economic Trinity *is* the immanent Trinity'.[1] I can only say that they all leave me in considerable doubt about this, and some more than others. For Rahner, the economic, free self-communication of the divine reality to Jesus, and the 'immanent' self-communication of the divine reality, are still two things, even if the dual purpose is described as 'two things at once'.[2] In Kasper much the same impression is given of the processing of the Spirit. He explicitly evokes the 'transcendental-condition-of-the-possibility-of' clause, the very hallmark, whether in this or in comparable phrasing, of the Platonic dualism within which most trinitarians still appear to be trapped. 'On the one hand, then,' says Kasper, 'the immanent love of God reaches its goal in the Spirit. But at the same time ... the love of God in the Spirit also moves beyond God himself,' and that constitutes the activity of God the Spirit in the world.[3] One begins to notice how frequently words like 'often', 'both' and 'too' occur even where Rahner's axiom rules.

Even Jüngel, who follows Moltmann in seeing the death of Jesus as the central 'economic' event in which the Trinity is revealed, cannot, for all his insistence in seeing only one event in God's 'coming to himself' and 'coming to us', avoid all impressions of duality. 'This death,' he writes, 'is the seal of that event in which God comes both to God and to man.'[4] And what of Moltmann himself on this matter? His is the intriguing suggestion that 'the economic Trinity completes and perfects itself to immanent Trinity when the history and experience of salvation are completed and perfected.'[5] This, if he meant it fully, could give acceptable substance to John McDade's reading of Jüngel, in which he argues that in Jüngel's trinitarian theology the events of the economy implement, effect, and finally confirm the relationality of the triune divine life.[6] But, of course, in view of the empirical fact that we are still on the way to full stature of sons of God, that God as Spirit has not yet brought everything 'in God' so that 'God is all in all', it follows that there is not now available to us any 'immanent' Trinity on which we could model our changing relationships; in fact there will be no immanent ('remaining in') Trinity properly speaking until all has returned 'in' to God, and God also, after a real history, will finally be all 'in' all of a real body, that of Jesus, and that of his extended 'body of Christ' in the world, and that of the extended body of those who make up the body of Christ, the physical world. Meanwhile, the only Trinity that is, and so the only Trinity that can be known, is that of the dynamic (the economy) in which the God that Jesus prayed to as Father, came into Jesus ('I am in the Father and the Father is in me'; 'God was in Christ reconciling the world to himself') and is still active in the world as the risen Lord Jesus, the life-giving Spirit (as Paul calls him in 1 Cor 15:45 – just the phrase used to describe the 'divinity' of the the Holy Spirit in the creed: the Lord and giver of life).

But is Moltmann happy to have his position described as such a move from a protological to an eschatological account of immanent Trinity? He must, of course, answer for himself. I can only say that when questioned on this point at the colloquium, he wished to make a distinction between doxological formulations and more general theological ones, and this leaves me with the impression that all of these contemporary theologians would have us operate with some presently available distinction between an immanent and an economic Trinity; and while we do so, the serious faults incurred by the new social models will continue to damage both our theology and our practical prospects.

What are these faults? First, there has been a great deal of bowdlerising of both scriptural and patristic materials, neither of which can ever be made to yield three immanent divine persons in even the minimum sense required for a social model. It would take far too long to illustrate this in detail, but one example of a common mistreatment of patristic material is worth giving. The social modelists appear to assume that if monarchy or undifferentiated monotheism predominates over a society of real persons in our imagery of the divine, imperial, if not indeed sexist types of authoritarianism, and consequent oppression of people, are bound to occur in human societies under such ideological influence. But this ignores both the more intelligent analyses of power (which can see it abused by such majorities in a democracy, as the Irish should know, as by sovereign monarchies or oligarchies) and more seriously, the liberating effects of Christians simply opposing to the lordship of Caesar, the sovereign lordship of the servant Jesus (after all, Tertullian's much maligned 'monarchy' principle was exercised in his view through, and only through, the 'economy' of Jesus and the Spirit of Jesus).

Second, charges of tritheism are never quite dropped, nor would it appear, can they be. It does not really matter how improved are the ideas of personhood with which we feel we can now operate as compared to less wise predecessors, or how superior these are thought to be in their understanding of the essentially relational nature of the process of becoming and of being a person. The fact of the matter remains that persons on these newer models can still be counted, and when these models are applied to immanent divine persons, there will be three of them in a way so similar to the sense in which there are three (or more) of us, that no subsequent enthusiasm for the relational unity of the three and no amount of emphasis on the uniqueness of a process which secures simultaneously unity and distinction in the coming to be of persons in community, can ever suffice to obviate a charge of tritheism. That much at least the Fathers knew and never forgot.

Additional moves made in recent trinitarian theology to avert the charge of tritheism are really futile. For example, Colin Gunton seems to think he will avoid that charge if he rejects the idea that the three persons have three wills, and talks instead of such interanimation of Father, Son and Spirit, that what is done is done by all three.[7] In fact, as John McDade unwittingly perhaps illustrates, such detailed stories are now being told about the interactive roles played by the Son and the Spirit in the immanent process of the former's 'generation' and the latter's 'spiration' (partly to reconcile East and West on the *filioque* problem), that social modelists could well find cover in quite generally conveyed impressions of three immanent gents up there, each with his own well-differentiated job to do, albeit all converging on the process of inter-relational person-forming. Perhaps what is happening now is that the social modelists are simply expressing the closet tritheism of so much of our uncritical impressions of the Christian Trinity, due in turn to our forgetfulness of what Rowan Williams called the rigorous and austere logic of the classical Patristic writers. In any case, it borders on the amusing to find David Brown upbraiding Gunton for his harshness towards Augustine, when Brown himself offers us the picture of three divine persons as three consciousnesses, each having a unique and different 'personal history' that we can actually envisage the other two persons being 'in full charge, as it were, of the running of the universe' during the (brief?) period when the Son of God was dead.[8]

At this point, of course, the enterprise of seeking a 'Trinity as a community of persons in relation' as a clue to 'a proper non-hierarchical understanding of society and the church and to our own and the divine relation to creation,' has resulted in such unadult--erated nonsense as to bring the whole of Christian theology into disrepute. On the one hand, Moltmann can hardly be blamed for these excesses of the social model; on the other, once one leaves open a possible distinction between immanent and economic Trinity, and with that the possibility of applying the things said of Jesus in the Scriptures to a 'second referent', an eternal Son of God who was a fully constituted person, as we know persons to be constituted, 'before' Jesus was conceived, then, at what point can you call a halt to a process which clearly can arrive at the plain nonsense which Brown had at the very least the courage to publish?

But I should like in conclusion to return to the ideological dangers of this social model of the Trinity; for whereas the alleged tritheisms may result in the end in no more than a relatively harmless piece of nonsense which only those who are paid to do so may be expected to read, the projection onto an immanent divine society of structures of social relationships destined thereafter for re-entry into our human task of building a better world can carry by this very detour an absolute normativeness and a foreclosure on other options, which are the hallmarks of ideology everywhere. I am intrigued, and better informed, when one of my students uses Levinas' *Otherwise than Being or Beyond Essence* in order to arrive at a truer understanding of the mutual vulnerability involved in the very coming-to-be of persons-in-relation; I can anticipate being even better informed when the call of one member of the colloquium for a finer, psychoanalytic analysis of personhood is answered; and I can simply discount the damage then done by trying to project these onto immanent divine persons, for I know that all these finer insights derived from watching real human persons. I will have all I need before that projection takes place, and I can use it in my own thinking about persons in relation. But when some concrete 'non-hierarchical understanding of society' is finally produced, and I remember Marx's statement that such religious visions are man's recognition of himself by a detour ('die Anerkennung des Menschens auf einem Umweg'), what will then protect me from the absolute claims which this vision will have picked up on its detour? Who will then allow me even a suspicion of its truth and finality, any more than the present hierarchs want to allow me.

Finally, then, if no substantial trace of an 'immanent' Trinity in any way distinct from an 'economic' Trinity is currently available to us, just what kind of trinitarian theology can we now have? Of what referents can it now be be composed?

The first referent is the God to whom Jesus prayed, calling him 'Father'. The second referent is Jesus of Nazareth, 'in' whom was this same God who was also in the world before Jesus, but who is now so much 'in' Jesus (and Jesus in God) as to enable us to say that in and through this human person of Jesus, God experiences a human destiny in the very process of shaping human destiny (saving, revealing).[9] The third referent – if it can really be called third, for at this point one realises that arithmetic has nothing to do with the matter – is now the same Jesus-Immanuel, but now as Risen Lord/life-giving Spirit of his 'body' in this world, this Jesus who was also in the world before this body, as the God active in and through him, was in the world before him.

We could use the same term for all three referents. God is Spirit; the risen Jesus is life-giving Spirit; the body of Christ is the life-giving Spirit still incarnate in the world, but now as community rather than individual, but still being brought by the indwelling Spirit, now in the 'character' of Jesus, to the fulness of grace and truth. Such use of terminology would give us a Spirit-Trinity, much as one finds in Paul if one reads, say, 1 Cor 12-15, paying particular attention to to 12:4-6 (the parallelism), 12:12-13 where 'members' are made into one body by being, as natural bodies are, animated by one Spirit, which, or who is identified in 15:45 as the 'second Adam', the risen Lord, Jesus. The word 'person' is not really apt as a name for naming all three referents simultaneously, for answering the question: three what? We believe the Father of our Lord Jesus Christ is a divine person, and Jesus is certainly a human person, but it would stretch the word 'person' beyond all recognisable content to go on to talk of three persons. As it always did, of course. Read Book 7 of Augustine's magisterial work on *The Trinity* , and watch the word person lose *all* that would enable it to describe a human person. So, in answer to the question: three what? First, refuse the rule of arithmetic, for a 'triadic' rather than a 'biadic' structure is suggested by the *history* of salvation, the economy itself in which God was before Jesus and Jesus before his 'body' in the world, rather than by any possible discovery of three divine persons in any way similar to a community of three (or more) human persons. Then, if absolutely necessary, take refuge in some such phrase as 'three modes of being' or 'modes of origin'(*tropoi hyparxeos*) of God, whose being is in becoming, and who becomes what God freely wills to be, the God who is all in all, in this very process known as the 'economy' (of salvation).

The term 'Spirit', of course, is not usually, and has not traditionally been used for all three, nor is there any reason why it should lay exclusive claim to that function, though it could well fulfill it. First, words such as 'Word' and the feminine 'Sophia' (Wisdom) are fully fledged alternatives, fully authorised in the common religious tradition of Jews and Greeks. It was, then, something of an accident of history that 'Word' was chosen by the first apologists as the cipher for the indwelling in Jesus, who recognised in it the obvious bridge-term for coming to grips with the dominant religious claims of the educated Greco-Roman world. Second, since each 'mode of being' reveals the same divine being (here is the need for the *homoousios*) as each other 'mode', and yet is not altogether identical with any other mode, a variety of terms is indicated as an alternative to a repetition of one term – so 'Word' and 'Spirit'.

In the patristic era, when Christian theologians borrowed all of the metaphysics for their Christologies, and ready-made 'binities' and 'trinities' from predominantly Platonic religious philosophers,[10] they naturally shared a dualist world-view and the ideal/empirical divisions of that era, and were thus prone to duplicate referents in just those ways which give us immanent in addition to economic Trinities. The best theologians of East and West, however, managed to find formulas to defeat the Arians (who in respect of Platonic dualism, were as prone to immanent divine speculation as themselves), without incurring the charge of tritheism. They did this with great difficulty – for the schemata borrowed from Porphyry and company were never designed for use of a person like Jesus – and in the end their relational formulae for immanent 'threes' were so abstruse as as to convey no conceivable information about the inner divine reality. So, if only by default, their successors were driven back to the story of Jesus and the history of his 'body' in the world, in order to find content for a divine revelation that would inspire and gradually improve; and trinitarian doctrine was left to slumber, seldom disturbed, in theology's back bedroom. That was not all a bad thing, one now recognises, especially when faced with modern efforts to renew the doctrine by trying to give it concrete relevance without exorcising the old dualism of ideal and empirical, immanent and economic. There are good reasons, then, to prefer Augustine's austere grammar of orthodoxy, utterly uninformative as it turns out to be on God's inner being, to any of the social models more recently produced.

Unless, of course, Rahner's axiom is finally taken in its fully radical sense: in the sense that we have only our economic Trinity, in the midst of which we now are, or half are. Then we are left to glean our vision for a better communal future in our extended body, this physical universe, from the concrete lessons that Jesus taught in his ways of relating to others and to things, in all of his life, death, and destiny. And that in turn is available to us, of course, only in the ongoing history of those scattered communities of his followers (and even outside of their formal boundaries), some of the earliest shapes of which is crystalised in the Scriptures. Furthermore, since this 'body' is still being built up to the point of God being all in all, to the stature of a fully immanent Trinity of God, Jesus and human community, and since it is quite blatantly nowhere near that happy consummation as yet, there is plenty of room for us to heed Professor Freyne's warning to us to pay more attention to *ta erkomena,* the things that are (yet) to come, as a result of Jesus's 'other paraclete' in the world; and there is no room at all for the crypto-ideologies that must always lurk in those social Trinities which have not quite abjured all knowledge of the inner being of God. Sustained fidelity to the rule of metaphor (the 'second' metaphor being: the followers of Jesus are the body of the divine Christ) must be one of the ways of achieving this happy result, though it is not, of course, the only way.

** This piece, delivered to the colloquium, was there described as part of a longer argument about the doctrine of the Trinity. The longer argument is due to appear under the title* Image and Metaphor in the Christian Understanding of God as Trinity, *in a Festschrift for D. W. D. Shaw (to be published shortly in Scotland). Our thanks are due to the editors for their agreement to publish this piece.*

1. Karl Rahner, *The Trinity* (London: Burns and Oates, 1970) 22
2. Ibid., 64.
3. Walter Kasper, *The God of Jesus Christ* (London: SCM Press, 1984) 226.
4. Eberhard Jüngel, *God as the Mystery of the World* (Edinburgh: T&T Clark, 1983) 383.
5. Jürgen Moltmann, *The Trinity and the Kingdom of God* (London: SCM Press, 1981) 161.
6. John McDade, *Pre-existence Language and the Dynamic of Metaphorical Predication* (Unpublished Ph.D. thesis, University of Edinburgh, 1986)
7. Colin Gunton, *The Promise of Trinitarian Theology* (Edinburgh: T&T Clark, 1991).
8. David Brown, *The Divine Trinity* (London: Duckworth, 1985).

See his review of Gunton's *The Promise of Trinitarian Theology* in *Theology*, March/April, 1992.

9. In short, God becomes human, incarnate; provided incarnation is not thought to refer merely to some moment of conception – becoming human takes a little longer than that – but refers to all of life and death and, if there is such, beyond death.

10. See John Dillon, 'Logos and Trinity: Patterns of Platonist Influence on Early Christianity' in G. Vesey, ed., *The Philosophy in Christianity* (Cambridge: CUP, 1989).

CHAPTER SEVEN

Feminist Theology and the Trinity

Ann Loades

Let me start by saying what I mean by the word 'feminist', as it bears many meanings, as do the words 'Christian' and 'theologian'. Feminism means simply a determination to secure change for the better in terms of justice for women. A feminist need not be female by sex; and not every female theologian is a feminist, that is to say, she does not necessarily have feminist issues at the top of her theological agenda. Nor may a feminist theologian expect that feminism will illuminate, let alone solve, every theological problem. To place oneself in this way along the spectrum of possibilities represented by feminism may well seem (at least initially) to be rather tame as compared with other positions. That it is not so tame can only be seen when one attempts to implement justice for women in the workplace, to even a small degree.

It is my workplace in a theology department which is the main focus of my attention, that institution, rather than my ecclesiastical community. I am distinctly fortunate in having another female colleague, though I do not think that we yet know quite how to evaluate the fact that it is both recent and still rare for women to be permitted to teach theology in a formal way. We can at least be grateful that there are university departments of theology in secular universities which make this possible for us. And then, mercifully spared the distress of a vocation to ordination in the Church of England, I could say that I have had another sort of vocation or role provided for me whether I like it or not. In other words, stay in the English university context and the role of being a statutory woman will be found, and that provides worries enough. Am I invited to do this, that, or the other in my own right, as it were, or not? Perhaps it is a good thing that I have to live without the answers. More important sometimes, is to ask the question whether I can afford to make a mess of something in the way some of my male colleagues quite clearly can, or will this have damaging consequences not only for me but for other women?

The apparent mildness of my feminism probably has much to do with distancing myself from my ecclesiastical institution, but it also has to do with the fact that my ecclesiastical environment happens to be an exceptionally privileged one. If I were less privileged I might be a lot angrier. I personally never have to cope with a level of incompetence in relation to women on the part of my pastors such as I recognise in the clerical caricatures of David Hare's *Racing Demon*, for example. This, I suspect, makes it possible for me to continue to find nurture in my particular ecclesiastical context (Durham cathedral) *despite* the fact that I am increasingly sensitive to the way in which both in its liturgy and its institutional life we all, women and men alike, have for the time being to cope with the exclusion, diminution and devaluation of women, even when they are not rendered wholly *invisible*.

Some of my dilemmas can be as readily articulated by articles in *The Times* as by reference to theology and liturgy. Writing for 10 March 1992, Janet Daley began by relating what she had to say on International Women's Day, just past. Rightly, she said that she found it insulting to be given a commemorative day as if she were part of some neglected minority or endangered species. Much as Dorothy Sayers had claimed half a century ago, Janet Daley insisted that women are half the population of the planet, and that being female is as much the predominant human experience as being male. Are we helped by 'reinforcing the view that women's needs are so separate from the usual run of things that their cause must be hyped, like those of Amazonian Indians or white whales?' There are certainly occasions when attention does need to be paid to women's needs, but one reason for the hype and for the 'ecumenical decade of churches in solidarity with women' or whatever, is that women all too often, as Janet Daley says, are not regarded (and worse, do not regard themselves) as real people. 'Self-effacing invisibility in public combined with sympathetic support in private is the ideal helpmeet face of the working woman.' Think of the *vinculum amoris*, the bond of love, the go-between glue role of the Spirit in some theology, and of course there's no problem in re-sexing or re-gendering the Spirit as 'she', is there?

To take another example from *The Times*, Libby Purvis on 13 April 1992, this time commenting on a European Community document about women which suggests that women at work want 'job satisfaction and human contact' while men want 'higher incomes and rapid promotion'. She is alert to the way in which 'the fearful hormones of motherhood do slosh around and cause unprofessional thoughts such as: "Poor old J.D., he looked like a lost little boy when I hit him with those figures, better back off".' Ms Macbeth too finds herself reaching out a helping hand to a young colleague with 'big troubled toddler eyes who will later stab her in the back.' Her concern overall, and rightly, is with the gender stereotyping which hinders the acknowledgement that plenty of men look for human contact and moral satisfaction at work, and that 'plenty of women wouldn't half mind a bit of fast promotion and serious money.' In theology, as in society, we are stuck with some gender-stereotyping – meaning by 'gender' what societies happen to make of the basic biological differences which identify some of us as female and some of us as male. Biology still matters – a point to which I'll return. No one lives free of gender roles, and a gender-free theology would, I suspect, be hard to find (unless we opt quite systematically for analogies for God which are as impersonal as we can make them), and I am unclear as to what it would be like to believe it, or to try to re-tell it or to teach it, let alone to live it. My main point here is that gender-constructions are astonishingly variable, and in the Christian tradition they are simply not variable enough. It's as though they've got stuck somewhere.

One which may be taken as representative is to be found in Nelle Mortin's book, *The Journey is Home* (1985). She describes a sculpture in wood outside a church building (Protestant, as it happens), a sculpture on the theme of vocation taken from 1 Cor 10: 31, 'Whether therefore ye eat, or drink, or whatsoever ye do, do all to the glory of God.' The sculpture shows thirty individual forms, representing nineteen different kinds of work. Only seven of the thirty figures are women, represented as nursing a baby, on knees scrubbing a floor, serving a man seated at table, assisting a male doctor, feeding chickens, pounding a typewriter, and teaching children. All these figures represent tasks that need doing (particularly nurturing the young – hence the need for attention to women's needs, so long as children are thought to be the responsibility of their mothers, rather than of their parents). It is absurd to exclude them from connection with the other twenty-three figures representing nineteen different kinds of work. It needs little imagination to think out the likely roles of the male figures in the sculpture. Is the gender construct of Christian theology for females to continue to associate them primarily, if not exclusively, with being passive, dependent, bodily, emotional, weak, peculiarly responsible for weakness and sin, childlike in the worst sense, and bearing the image of God only derivatively? Is the gender construction for males to continue to be that they are active, independent, intelligent, brave, strong, good, bear the image of God in their own right, and are of course godlike? Is it really impossible to learn to value human differences appropriately, and to avoid locating all those associated with males/masculinity at the top of some hierarchy of value, with those associated with females/femininity at the bottom? Could we not learn to appreciate that passivity, dependence, bodiliness, emotion, acknowledging weakness, etc. are arguably as important aspects of being human as being active, brave, independent and so on?

One might think that this does not connect with the ways we think theologically, but regrettably it does. Take, for example, the words of a bishop arguing that 'in the whole of human instinct and understanding it is the masculine which is associated with giving and the feminine with receiving'. Quite apart from its accidental 'lie back and think of England' undertones, this is manifestly false as a description in my view – men and women simply do not relate to one another in this simplistic way; and it is thoroughly bad as prescription – if human beings try to relate to one another like this, disaster can, and does follow. Each needs to give and receive from one another in as open and reciprocal ways as they can.

Implicit, and unexamined in the bishop's mind, is a fundamental assumption which pervades our doctrines, liturgies and institutions, an assumption not unique to the Christian tradition but well worked into it, and it has to do with a particular understanding of 'paternity'. We have known for a century and a half that it is false – it is the belief that it is males who are primarily creative, or pro-creative, that the male has the primary and essential role in reproduction, and that a child originates from one source. We can say until we are blue in the face that God (not being like a human person) transcends both sex and gender, but that is not how our existing symbol patterns seem to work. Male/masculine metaphor is given pride of place, understandably, if we believe that males are godlike procreators, and women merely exist to nurture them and 'their' offspring. So the British Council of Churches study commission on trinitarian doctrine, in its report *The Forgotten Trinity,* suggests we should base 'the being of God' in the Father as the 'personal basis' of deity. Another example can be found in the Apostolic Letter of John Paul II *On the Dignity and Vocation of Woman* (1988) which desperately tries to cope with the new understanding, that procreation is a joint project of women and men together, hitched uneasily to the old understanding of paternity (p. 30).

There must come a point when we frankly acknowledge that we cannot put up with this sort of thing anymore, and must ask whether parent-metaphors for God (even of the motherly-father sort) are not now too problematic. Beyond that, it must also be acknowledged that female/feminine related metaphor for God, *in, of and by itself,* is as appropriate or inappropriate, or as adequate or inadequate for God as the male/masculine.

Feminist theology would, I believe, insist on this point, but ultimately wants to put itself out of business by affirming that we find ways of talking about God which would move us well beyond this kind of issue. Why can we not give serious weight to the argument that the very incomprehensibility of God demands a proliferation of images, and a variety of names, each of which acts as a corrective against the tendency of any particular one to become reified and literal? (See E. Clapsis, 'Naming God: An Orthodox View', *The Ecumenical Review* 44:1, 1992, 100-112). That sort of move could in principle shift us out of the difficulties with which some of us struggle, and make it possible for us to live without devaluing women on theological grounds.

CHAPTER EIGHT

Some Implications of Cosmology for Our Understanding of God as Creator

Gabriel Daly

Today's ecological crisis is perhaps the principal stimulus to a renewed interest in the Christian theology of creation. This circumstance, however, for all its urgency, should not divert us from the realisation that such an interest was long overdue anyway. When theologians handed nature over to the scientists in the 17th and 18th centuries, they were merely reinforcing a direction which had been taken in Western theology centuries earlier: creation had long since become little more than a backdrop to redemption.

One result of leaving nature to the scientists is that Christian theology has remained curiously untouched, until recently, by relativity theory, quantum mechanics, or Hubble's discovery of the red shift, to mention the three great 20th century scientific developments which Ernan McMullin has pointed to as the begetters of modern cosmology. I mention McMullin, partly because he has done some valuable pioneering work in the history of science and its relevance to theology, but mainly because ten years ago he wrote that on the whole theologians were not disposed to think of cosmology as having much relevance for theology. He made quite clear his conviction that this was rather remiss of them.[1]

This situation is, I think, changing, largely as the result of the need felt by theologians to make an appropriate response to the ecological crisis. Most theologians are not professionally competent as scientists. (I am among them.) But we cannot afford to make this an excuse for not taking a subject like cosmology with theological seriousness. Fortunately there are professional scientists writing for the general reader, just as there are professional scientists who are also practising theologians.

Ian Barbour has pointed out that 'Our understanding of God's relation to nature always reflects our view of nature'.[2] Neither the Ptolemaic, Copernican, nor Newtonian universes lent themselves to a theology of divine presence or sustained action in the world. Indeed, Newton's universe seems tailor-made for deistic absenteeism (mitigated by the occasional divine visit to shore up a sagging planetary orbit here, or to rectify the direction of a wayward comet there).

Nature, as revealed to us through quantum theory and evolutionary biology, is a strange blend of unpredictable and random events and a statistical regularity sufficient to allow one to speak of its laws.

Niels Bohr, echoing Augustine's reflection on the mind in search of God, remarked that those who were not shocked when they first came across quantum physics could not possibly have understood it.[3] One appreciates his point. Literally unimaginable indeterminate smudges of energy wait to be observed in order to achieve concrete existence. The observer is part of the observed phenomenon. Yet observation is itself limited to mutually exclusive modes: you can determine the position of an electron but only at the expense of being able to measure or observe its momentum. The sub-atomic world is composed of potentialities whose actualization is not pre-determined, except in a broad statistical sense. Sub-atomic particles are not individual solitary entities but belong to a system within which they interact mysteriously and unpredictably with each other. It now appears that more than fideistic believers are saying 'Credo quia absurdum'; and one does not have to be a Kierkegaardian to embrace the paradox: particle physicists are doing it every day.

This new humility imposed by events on scientists may give some encouragement to those theologians who realize what has happened. There are, however, dangers here. Shared epistemological discomfort is not a promising basis for interdisciplinary cooperation.

Newtonian determinism was a major casualty of the new physics. Pierre de Laplace had claimed that if the position and motion of every particle in the universe were known with exactitude at one instant, it would be possible to compute the entire past and future history of the universe.[4] Laplace's appalling thesis remains attractive to some scientific minds when faced with phenomena which resist rational explanation, just as its theological equivalent has often been invoked by believers who want to ascribe every event to the direct intervention of God.

On the other hand it is easy to appreciate why theologians of a different cast of mind might warm to quantum theory. When Heisenberg remarks that 'even in science the object of research is no longer nature itself, but man's investigation of nature',[5] he sounds so like Schleiermacher and the liberal Protestant tradition that one can't help wondering whimsically whether physics will throw up a scientific equivalent of Karl Barth sternly calling it back from its Copenhagen exile.

In the meantime we can rejoice in a God who is apparently happy to be creative, at both microscopic and macroscopic level, through the instrumentality of an elegant interplay between chance and necessity.[6]

It is easy to underestimate the challenge that this kind of thinking offers to much traditional Christian spirituality and theology. In terms of spirituality it removes the comfort of aligning oneself with the undoubted will of God manifested in a nature which responds directly and immediately to that will in every instance, just as it is manifested in God's permission of human evil in the world. Augustine, reflecting on how God gave power to pagan emperors and kings and permitted evil to happen to Christians during Alaric's sack of Rome in 410, admits to puzzlement but finally concludes: 'Manifestly these things are ruled and governed by the one God according as he pleases; and if his motives are hidden, are they therefore unjust?'[7] Augustine's theodicy is the theological equivalent of Laplace's imperfectly understood universe. The approach is similar, for all that one is a believer and the other an unbeliever: if you could see the whole canvas you would also see that things could not be otherwise.

In a sense, the quest for a Theory of Everything is an exercise in secular eschatology. The search presupposes faith in the existence of the goal; and the goal, for some at least, is the possibility of explaining the cosmos without reference to a transcendent creator, on the curious grounds that the discovery of a Grand Unified Theory will demonstrate the lack of need to postulate the existence of such a creator.

Quantum theory nevertheless raises serious questions for traditional theology. How does one take the quantum world into one's theological reckoning without falling into deism? A new model of divine immanence in creation is needed to fit a situation where sub-atomic events are intrinsically unpredictable except in terms of a broad statistical probability.

It may very well be that process thought, in one or other of its forms, is a necessary, if perhaps temporary, stage in the journey from an undue reliance on essentialist, existentialist, or historicist types of theological thinking. At any rate it would appear that many of the theologians who have come from a professional scientific background have a marked interest in process thought. Ian Barbour notes that process thought is 'particularly compatible' with modern cosmology, since it is disposed to see 'reality [as] constituted by events and relationships rather than by separate substances or separate particles'.[8] It is holistic and sees nature in relational terms, and it makes becoming rather than being a central category of its thinking. Some theologians are uneasy about its affirmation that creation belongs to the nature of God. Others see its thesis of dipolarity as trying to have one's cake and eat it. Others again take issue with its rejection of creation *ex nihilo* and its substitution for it of creation out of chaos.

One of the attractive features of process thought is that it gives nearly everybody something to disagree with. At any rate, taking cosmology with theological seriousness makes it virtually impossible to avoid engaging with process thought, however guardedly.

Another benefit of the new physics is that by promoting holistic thinking it acts as a powerful corrective to the sterile reductionism which is endemic in certain types of scientific thought. In addition, it has bequeathed to theology the heuristic and hermeneutical device of the *model*, which allows one to practise negative theology without having to take a vow of total silence. This may or may not be thought a blessing, but it is an undeniable fact of theological life, at least in the English-speaking world.

Some theologians have actually applied Niels Bohr's theory of complementarity to the classical christological and trinitarian doctrines. Here, however, it would be wise to heed John Hedley Brooke in his recent book, *Science and Religion: Some Historical Perspectives,* when he warns against incautious use of the new physics by theologians. Complementarity in physics applies to two descriptions of the same phenomenon, each of which is complete in itself, though exclusive of the other when measured or observed. 'To switch from complementarity at the same level to complementarity between different levels (especially if one involved the transcendent) [is] not a straightforward move.'[9]

There is also the danger of circular argument. Bohr turned to psychology and philosophy for support of his scientific theory. For example, he drew on William James's notion of the stream of consciousness: if you try to examine the stream of consciousness, it ceases, by that very fact, to be what you want to examine. Bohr also took inspiration from Kierkegaard's protest against the objectivizing effect of scientism and Hegelianism. Human beings are subjects not objects. Brooke comments drily: 'With so rich an input into the Copenhagen interpretation of quantum mechanics, it is not surprising that religious apologists should obtain an output. But the danger of circularity is transparent.'[10]

What cosmology forces insistently on the theologian's attention is the inherently insoluble problem of the mode of God's action in the world. Here, if anywhere, negative theology rules. It is not a Laplacean lack of relevant evidence or an insufficiently evolved brain power which makes this an intrinsically insoluble problem. Recognition of our inability to understand God's action in causal terms is an integral and scandalizing feature of faith. Yet seeking to deny that there is any efficient causality in God's relationship with the world on the grounds that efficient causality necessarily trenches on freedom or is unacceptably patriarchal is, I think, unreal. Causality, thus banished, inevitably returns under another name. Surely it is better to accept the paradox of affirming *both* divine causality on the one hand *and* chance and freedom on the other. There seems little to be gained by making the word 'creation' theologically correct while banishing the word 'cause' as theologically unacceptable. Instead, given that models have become a fact of theological life, we might as well lay on a plentiful supply of them on the grounds that, as Ian Ramsey liked to say, there is safety in numbers.

A final reflection on the beneficial influence of cosmology on the Christian theology of creation concerns its value as a corrective to the anthropocentrism which is endemic in traditional theology. Existentialism, the principal twentieth century alternative to Scholasticism, intensified the anthropocentrism which was already present. Rudolf Bultmann's opinion that humanity is radically separate from the cosmos is a reminder that his stratagem for dealing with modernity is in line with Schleiermacher's expedient in respect of religion and science expressed in an open letter to Lücke in which he gave it as his aim in writing his *Doctrine of Faith* to show 'that every dogma truly representing an element of our Christian awareness can also be formulated in such a way that it leaves us uninvolved with science.'[11]

Viewing uninvolvement with science as a theological virtue is a characteristcally Enlightenment perspective. The Galileo affair had suggested, to both unbelievers and critically minded believers alike, that the further theologians could be kept from scientific matters, the better for all concerned. Today, however, an increasing number of theologians appreciate the need for an interdisciplinary link with science in general and with cosmology in particular. For most of the time the move towards dialogue will have to come from the religious side, since scientists who are not believers have no compelling reasons for taking the initiative and a fair amount of prejudice to conquer even in responding to one.

One still encounters some theological resistance to this turn to science. John Macquarrie, in his influential book, *Principles of Christian Theology*, seems to echo Schleiermacher when he expresses a fear that approaching creation through nature rather than exclusively through humanity 'can so easily become the question of how things began and can trespass into an area that properly belongs to science'.[12] ('Properly' here seems to mean 'exclusively'.) If this means, for example, that there is a danger of identifying the moment of creation, theologically considered, with the Big Bang, then, of course, his point is well taken. One might have hoped, however, that critically-minded theologians have learnt enough from past mistakes to avoid such crudities of correlation.

Existentialist theologians have tended towards anthropocentrism, not only from a fear of involvement with science, but also because existentialism is of its very nature anthropocentric in its analysis of *Dasein* and in its preoccupation with authenticity. However understandable such human-centredness may be as a reaction against scientism and essentialism, it is becoming increasingly difficult to accept that '...our first step toward an interpretation of the doctrine of creation is to take man himself rather than nature as the paradigm of creaturely beings.'[13]

The plain truth today is that the ecological crisis is teaching us that we can no longer afford our customary anthropocentrism and that our theology of creation must now be focused upon nature, with human beings as the most complex development of, and within, nature. At any rate, quite apart from ecological stimuli, the fact that cosmologists are talking about the mind of God is perhaps an indication of the direction in which theologians ought to be venturing – risks notwithstanding.

Notes

1. E. McMullin, 'How Should Cosmology Relate to Theology?' in A.R. Peacocke, ed., *The Sciences and Theology in the Twentieth Century* (Stocksfield: 1981) 17.
2. I. Barbour, *Religion in an Age of Science* (London: 1990) 183.
3. See Barbour, op.cit., 95-101 for a succinct comment on quantum theory.
4. C. Kaiser, *Creation and the History of Science* (London: 1991) 267-9.
5. J. H. Brooke, *Science and Religion: Some Historical Perspectives* (Cambridge: 1991) 334.
6. See D.J. Bartholomew, *God of Chance* (London: 1984). See also A.R. Peacocke, *Theology for a Scientific Age: Being and Becoming – Natural and Divine* (Oxford: 1990) 115-21.
7. Augustine, *De Civitate Dei* , V, 21.
8. Barbour, *Religion in an Age of Science*, 221.
9. Brooke, *Science and Religion*, 331.
10. ibid, 333.
11. Cited in K. Barth, *Protestant Theology in the Nineteenth Century: Its Background and History* (London: 1972) 445.
12. J. Macquarrie, *Principles of Christian Theology* (London: 1977) 216.
13. Macquarrie, *Principles*, 212.

CHAPTER NINE

Wittgenstein and the Irrationality of Rational Theology

Vincent Brümmer

1. *Rational Theology*

According to Anthony Kenny, 'some theologians regard religion as a way of life which can only be understood by participation and therefore cannot be justified to an outsider on neutral rational grounds. Such people must consider any attempt at a philosophical proof of God's existence to be wrong-headed ... To me it seems that if belief in the existence of God cannot be rationally justified, there can be no good grounds for adopting any of the traditional monotheistic religions'.[1] Clearly, for Kenny a rational theology providing a successful philosophical proof for God's existence is a *conditio sine qua non* for the acceptability of any form of theistic religion.

These sentiments are shared by Richard Swinburne according to whom a theist can be defined a 'a man who believes that there is a God' since the 'central core of theistic belief' is the proposition 'that God exists, that there is a God'.[2] Unlike Kenny, however, Swinburne is confident about the possibility of a rational theology which can not only show that a theistic concept of God is logically coherent, but can also demonstrate the truth of the proposition that such a God exists and thereby provide the required rational justification of theistic belief. In his book on *The Existence of God*, Swinburne argues in detail that the traditional philosophical arguments for the existence of God, corroborated by the testimony of religious experience, provide a rational justification for the theist's belief in the likelihood of God's existence. 'On our total evidence theism is more probable than not.'[3]

In this paper I would like to argue that for two reasons the kind of rational theology demanded by Kenny and provided by Swinburne is misguided and unreasonable. First of all, Kenny's denial of the view that religious belief is primarily a way of life, combined with Swinburne's claim that its 'central core' is belief in the proposition 'that there is a God', entails the abstraction of belief in the existence of God from the religious 'form of life' in which it is embedded and the 'language game' in which the latter is expressed. Like all propositions, the claim that God exists derives its meaning from the language-game within which it is asserted. Divorced from this context it is either misconstrued or meaningless. Secondly, the kind of rational theology which Kenny requires and Swinburne tries to provide, is impossible in principle since the claim that God exists is not the sort of claim which can be proved or disproved in the required sense. Taken by itself, apart from the religious form of life in which it is embedded, it is in an important sense neither verifiable nor falsifiable in experience. In Popperian terms, we could say that it is a metaphysical presupposition and not a scientific hypothesis since it is in principle compatible with whatever happens in the empirical world.[4] For this reason all attempts to show that the existence of God could be logically inferred from empirical evidence or logically contradicted by such evidence, could be shown to be circular: they all implicitly presuppose what they try to prove. The existence of God can only be inferred from experience which has first been interpreted in the light of the belief that God exists, and it can only be contradicted by experience which has first been interpreted in the light of the belief that there is no such God. For these two reasons, rational theology misconstrues the nature of both theistic belief and its atheistic denial. But what then is the nature of the claim that God exists, and in what sense is there still room for a debate between religious believers and non-believing outsiders? Is Kenny not justified in his suspicion that there cannot be any 'neutral rational grounds' on which such a debate could take place?

Let us try to deal with these issues by interpreting the claim that God exists as an example of what Wittgenstein calls a 'tacit presupposition' which is constitutive for a 'form of life'. As such it stands or falls with the meaningfulness of the form of life which it constitutes: if we accept the form of life, we logically cannot doubt or deny the claim which constitutes it. Divorced from the form of life in which it is embedded, the claim has no meaning at all. Taken as a hypothesis of which the probability can be proved or disproved apart from the form of life, the claim that God exists is misconstrued and loses its meaning. A rational debate about the truth or falsehood of such a claim is therefore misguided and irrational.

This Wittgensteinian interpretation of religious belief needs further elaboration. Let us start by explaining what Wittgenstein means by a 'form of life' and by the 'language game' in which it is expressed, and showing how religion could be understood as a form of life. Then we will explain what Wittgenstein means by 'tacit presuppositions' which constitute a form of life, and show how the existence of God could be understood as a tacit presupposition constitutive for the religious form of life. After that we will try to remove the common misunderstanding that the application of these Wittgensteinian terms to religious belief entails an absurd form of fideism which makes it impossible to discuss religious beliefs with outsiders. In conclusion we will try to spell out the implications of this view for the nature and the task of theology and for the possibility of a dialogue about the tenability of theistic belief

2. *Language-games and forms of life*

Unfortunately the meaning of Wittgenstein's term 'language-game' is far from clear. As with many other key terms in his writings, he fails to provide a detailed systematic development of it, and his rather cryptic and often aphoristic remarks give rise to much speculation and a large variety of proposed interpretations in the Wittgenstein literature. Wittgenstein himself defines the term as 'the whole, consisting of language and the actions into which it is woven'.[5] This suggests that language-games are primarily forms of action involving the use of language. Wittgenstein states that his use of the term 'is meant to bring into prominence the fact that the speaking of language is part of an activity, or a form of life'.[6] But what does he mean by a 'form of life'?

George Pitcher explains the term 'form of life' in the light of Wittgenstein's remark that 'if a lion could talk, we could not understand him'.[7] Of this Pitcher writes as follows: 'Suppose a lion says "It is now three o'clock", but without looking at a clock or his wrist-watch – and we may imagine that it would be merely a stroke of luck if he should say this when it actually is three o'clock. Or suppose he says "Goodness, it is three o'clock; I must hurry to make that appointment", but he continues to lie there, yawning, making no effort to move, as lions are wont to do. In these circumstances – assuming that the lion's general behaviour is in every respect exactly like that of an ordinary lion, save for his amazing ability to utter English sentences – we could not say that he has asserted or stated that it is three o'clock, even though he has uttered suitable words. We could not tell what, if anything, he has asserted, for the modes of behaviour into which his use of words is woven are too radically different from our own. We could not understand him, since he does not share the relevant forms of life with us.'[8] Of course this lion is very different from speaking animals occurring in children's stories. In Kenneth Grahame's *The Wind in the Willows* we can understand the Rat, the Mole, the Badger and the Toad since they do not merely utter English sentences. While doing so, they also behave as Englishmen do when uttering these sentences, and not like rats, moles, badgers and toads. Clearly, then, the meaning of a linguistic expression is its use within the form of life which forms the context within which it is uttered. Divorced from the form of life it is meaningless. We can only understand what someone says when we interpret it within the context of the form of life within which it is said. Furthermore, if we were to interpret it in terms of some other form of life, the result would be conceptual confusion. Gilbert Ryle would say that we are committing a 'category mistake'.

For Wittgenstein religious belief can be viewed as a specific form of life in which people participate. It is the form of life in which religious believers try to make sense of their lives and their experience of the world around them by relating life and the world to God in terms of the metaphors and conceptual models derived from their religious tradition: My life is meaningful because God loves me and I am a child of God, and the world around me is meaningful because it has been created by God his wonders to proclaim, etc., etc. In order to partake in this form of life, we need to be introduced into the language-game expressing it and into the use of the metaphors and models which characterise it. In this connection Wittgenstein says that we have to learn 'the technique of using a picture.'[9] It is part of the task of theology to explain this technique to us by making explicit the implicit 'conceptual grammar' of the religious language-game and of the use of the pictures employed in it. If we know the logical limits of the religious language-game we are able to distinguish it from other language-games and avoid the conceptual confusion which results from ignoring the differences between them.

The 'logical limits' to the use of a religious picture have to do with the inferences which can or cannot be validly drawn from it within the religious language-game. I master the technique of using the picture when I know which inferences I can and cannot draw from it. Wittgenstein illustrates this point in the light of the picture: God's eye sees everything. Which inferences could a believer draw from this picture, and which inferences would be invalid within the religious language game? Obviously, a believer would say that, since God's eye sees everything, God is aware of all that happens, not only in the world but also in the hearts and minds of all people: 'Almighty God, unto whom all hearts be open, all desires known, and from whom no secrets are hid ... ' However, Wittgenstein asks the rhetorical question: 'Are eyebrows going to be talked of, in connection with the Eye of God?'[10] Here we have clearly reached the 'logical limits' of the picture. It is conceivable that a child might ask after the eyebrows of God. It is however part of the child's introduction to the religious language-game to learn that such a question is out of order since it transgresses the 'logical limits' of the language-game. For this reason the catechism not only teaches us to give the right answers but also to ask the right questions! There is a second kind of inference which we must also learn to draw if we are to master the technique. Since the religious language-game is embedded in the religious form of life, using the religious picture entails that we commit ourselves to this form of life. Saying 'almighty God, unto whom all hearts be open, all desires known, and from whom no secrets are hid... ', commits the speaker to a complex set of feelings, attitudes and actions which follow from looking on life in the world in terms of this picture. Uttering these words without uttering the entailed commitment, would be as absurd as the yawning lion who *says* that he must hurry to keep his appointment while making no effort to move. Such commissive implications are also an essential part of the conceptual grammar of the religious language-game. Understanding the language-game is only possible if we know how to participate in the form of life in which it is embedded, and if we know how this form of life differs from, and is related to, all the other forms of life in which we might participate.

Wittgenstein admits that religious 'pictures' have a commissive force: using them commits us to the religious form of life expressed through them. Do they also have a constative force? Does the language-game of religion require that they should in some way also be claimed to be factually true? According to W.D. Hudson, 'what Wittgenstein ... seems at times to have come near to suggesting is that, because religious beliefs have commissive force, that somehow entitles us to bypass the troublesome problem of their constative force.'[11] However, Wittgenstein's remarks on the tacit presuppositions which are constitutive for a language-game, seem to point in another direction.

3. Tacit presuppositions

Wittgenstein introduces the term 'tacit presupposition' in the context of some remarks on behaviourism in Philosophical Investigations (II, p. 179-180). In these remarks he makes use of the following example: if a doctor hears the groaning of a patient, he *tacitly presupposes* that the groaning is an expression of pain. However, he cannot feel the patient's pain himself. A behaviourist might reject this tacit presupposition as being empirically unverifiable, and would therefore look on the patient merely as an object exhibiting groan-behaviour. This behaviour could be terminated by treating the patient with analgesic. In rejecting the tacit presupposition, however, the behaviourist also takes leave of the form of life of personal relations, since the presupposition that you have feelings, emotions etc., even though I cannot myself experience them, is logically constitutive for my treating you as a person rather than as an object.

Treating somebody else as a person also presupposes that the other is a free agent in the sense of being the initiator of his own actions and hence having the ability to have done other than he did.[12] Since this is a counterfactual presupposition, it is also not empirically verifiable: I can only observe what you do in fact and not that you could have acted differently from the way in which you acted in fact! The determinist who rejects this counterfactual presupposition, also takes leave of the form of life of personal relations, since the presupposition is logically constitutive for this form of life and for the language-game embedded in it. Since such tacit presuppositions are in this way *logically constitutive* for the language-game, they cannot be doubted or denied *within* the language-game itself. Doubting or denying them would entail doubting or denying the language-game as such.

In a similar way P.F. Strawson argues that the presupposition that the material objects which we observe around us continue to exist at times when there is nobody to observe them, is logically constitutive for the language-game of science and of our common-sense dealings with the world. The sceptic who doubts this presupposition 'pretends to accept a conceptual scheme, but at the same time quietly rejects one of the conditions for its employment. Thus his doubts are unreal, not because they are logically irresoluble doubts, but because they amount to a rejection of the whole conceptual scheme within which alone such doubts make sense.'[13]

Something similar happens to all our illocutionary acts.[14] These too are constituted by presuppositions about the nature of the world. Thus I cannot (logically) make a promise without presupposing that I will be able to fulfil my promise, and I cannot (logically) request someone else to do something while denying that the other has the ability to do what I ask. Making a promise or a request while at the same time denying that the promise or request can be fulfilled, is as absurd as someone who *says* agitatedly that he must hurry to keep an appointment while at the same time continuing to lie lazily in the sun.

Similarly the claim that God exists can be understood as a constitutive presupposition of the form of life in terms of which the theist makes sense of life and experience, and of the language-game in which this is expressed. Within the language-game this presupposition cannot be doubted or denied since denying it would entail taking leave of the form of life as such. This explains why the existence of God is a 'necessary truth' for the believer.[15] In this sense we could agree with J. N. Findlay's contention that for the believer partaking in the religious form of life, God's 'non-existence must be wholly unthinkable in any circumstances. There must, in short, be no conceivable alternative to an existence properly called 'divine': God must be wholly inescapable ... whether for thought or reality.'[16] Doubting or denying the existence of God or looking on it as a conjecture of which the relative likelihood or unlikelihood could somehow be established, would be quite absurd within the language-game of religious belief. Clearly

Swinburne's conclusion that 'on our total evidence theism is more probable than not'[17] should strike the believer as decidedly odd.

In this respect religious beliefs are quite different from scientific theories which remain conjectures which are always subject to methodical doubt and empirical refutation. Religious beliefs are not open to doubt or refutation within the context of the form of life itself, any more than the constitutive presuppositions of science are open to scientific doubt or refutation.[18] According to Wittgenstein, the demand that religious beliefs should be subject to empirical verification or falsification, is based upon conceptual confusion. With reference to Father O'Hara's attempt to make religious belief into 'a question of science' which can be verified on the basis of scientific evidence, Wittgenstein says: 'I would definitely call O'Hara unreasonable. I would say, if this is religious belief, then it is all superstition.'[19] The unreasonableness of the demand that religious beliefs should conform to the rules and fulfil the point of scientific hypothesis, is well expressed by W.D. Hudson: 'But "How is this religious belief to be empirically falsified?" is a pseudo problem – like, "How many runs did Bobby Charlton score in the World Cup?" And, unless you have decided in advance that cricket is the only game worth playing, the fact that this latter question is nonsensical does not imply that soccer is worthless. Nor does it follow that theological belief is meaningless or disreputable, if it is not a scientific hypothesis. A pro- or anti- apologetic which supposes that it does is simply wrong-headed.'[20]

Divorced from the religious language-game and its form of life, the claim that God exists becomes superfluous and loses all significance. Thus we could say that religious beliefs are internal to the religious form of life. This explains the sense in which religious beliefs are necessarily *existential* : they are internally connected to the way religious believers make sense of their lives and experience and therefore cannot be viewed in abstraction from the meaning of their very existence. It makes sense to say: 'I know that Jupiter exists and is the largest planet in our solar system, but I could not care less about that.' It would, however, be absurd to say: 'I know that God exists and is the Creator of heaven and earth, but I could not care less about that.'

This Wittgensteinian way of understanding the status of the claim that God exists, could call up some serious misunderstandings. In the first place, it should be noted that the constitutive propositions of a language-game refer to the *factual nature* of the world within which the language-game is to be played. It would be absurd to participate in a language-game without presupposing that the factual nature of the world is such that the form of life to which the language-game commits us and in which it is embedded, can be realised within the world. As we have argued above, commitments are constituted by the presupposition that the factual state of the world is such that these commitments can be fulfilled within the world. This also applies to those constitutive presuppositions which are metaphysical and therefore neither verifiable nor falsifiable empirically. It is at this point that I part company with a Wittgenstein interpreter like D.Z. Philips.[21] He would agree with me that belief in God's existence is a constitutive presupposition of the theistic form of life and in this sense internal to it. Nevertheless, unlike me he would interpret this belief in a non-realistic way. For him it cannot be a *factual* belief since that would require it to be empirically verifiable or falsifiable apart from the form of life in which it is embedded and thus turn it into an empirical hypothesis external to the form of life. This merely shows that he implicitly holds to an old-fashioned verificationist definition of the term 'factual'. Indeed, if 'factual' means 'empirically verifiable or falsifiable', the belief that God exists is not factual! But do we need to accept this definition of 'factual'? Doing so would make nonsense of all forms of life (like those referred to above) which are constituted by metaphysical presuppositions about the nature of the world. As we have pointed out above, it would be absurd to participate in a form of life without presupposing that the *factual* nature of the world is such that this form of life can be realised within the world.[22]

This is well illustrated by the following example which is perfectly in accordance with Wittgenstein's views on tacit presuppositions: 'If I say "The Lord is my strength and shield", and if I am a believer, I may experience feelings of exultation and be confirmed in an attitude of quiet confidence. If, however, I tell myself that the arousal of such feelings and confirming of attitude is *the* function of the sentence, that despite appearances it does not refer to a state of affairs, then the more I reflect on this the less I shall exult and the less appropriate my attitude will seem. For there was no magic in the sentence by virtue of which it mediated feelings and confirmed attitudes: these were *responses* to the kind of Being to whom, I trusted, the sentence referred: and response is possible only so long as that exists to which or to whom the response is made.'[23] Clearly, then, understanding the meaning of life and the world in terms of theistic models presupposes belief in the factual truth of these models. Conceptual models fail to provide the understanding sought for in religion if they are taken to be merely useful fictions and not in some sense 'reality depicting'.[24] In other words, religious faith entails some form of critical realism[25] regarding the ontological status of religious models or 'pictures'.

4. Fideism

A second misunderstanding which might be called up by this Wittgensteinian interpretation of religious belief, is the following: although the constitutive presuppositions of a language-game cannot be doubted or denied *within* the context of the language-game itself, this does not mean that the language-game as such is somehow immunized against doubt and rejection. To a greater or lesser extent the forms of life in which language-games are embedded, are all subject to historical and cultural change. Changes in the factual circumstances of our lives and in the problems and demands with which life confronts us, give rise to changes in our culture and thus also in the forms of thought which we find adequate, the language-games in which these forms of thought find expression and in the concomitant beliefs which we hold to be true. The more we become aware of the cultural differences between different times and places, the more we realise the untenability of the Platonic view that human thought is essentially timeless and immutable. Because of changes in the demands of life, our forms of thought can never remain adequate for all time. In this sense we can understand Wittgenstein's claim that the multiplicity of language-games 'is not something fixed, given once and for all; but new types of language, new language-games, as we may say, come into existence, and others become obsolete and forgotten.'[26] Elsewhere Wittgenstein illustrates this point as follows: 'Earlier physicists are said to have found suddenly that they had too little mathematical understanding to cope with physics; and, in almost the same way, young people today can be said to be in a situation where ordinary common sense no longer suffices to meet the strange demands life makes. Everything has become so intricate that mastering it would require an exceptional intellect. Because skill at playing the game is no longer enough; the question that keeps coming up is: can this game be played at all now and what is the right game to play?'[28]

Witttgenstein clearly admits that language-games, and the forms of life in which they are embedded, can be contested in the light of the changing demands of life. Since this also applies to religious forms of life, every 'fideistic' interpretation of Wittgenstein, like that put forward by Kai Nielsen,[28] is excluded at this point. In other words, although religions can be characterised in Wittgensteinian terms as 'language-games embedded in forms of life', this in no way entails that they are self-enclosed autonomous monads which are immune from external criticism.[29] The so-called 'Wittgensteinian fideism' is by no means Wittgensteinian.

Of course not all language-games are to the same extent subject to change.[30] Thus some language-games are so bound up with our lives as personal beings that they cannot be rejected without giving up all forms of life involving personal relations. Such relations would be impossible without, for example, such elementary illocutionary activities as making factual assertions, promises and requests, and expressing our beliefs, intentions, feelings, expectations, etc. It is hard to imagine the sort of changes in the circumstances of our lives which would make these obsolete. This could only come to pass if all human beings were somehow turned into impersonal robots related to each other causally rather than personally. Although this might be imaginable in science fiction, it is hardly likely in the real world. There are, however, other language-games, including forms of religion, which can become obsolete through changes in the circumstances of our lives. A good example is that of the ancient fertility cults in the Mediterranean basin, which were so strongly embedded in an agrarian way of life, that they could not survive the rise of trade, industry and the urbanisation of society. They proved quite inadequate as a means of making sense of these changed circumstances in the lives of people.[31] Other language-games, however, allow for amendment and creative reinterpretation by means of which they can remain adequate to the changing demands of life. To a greater or lesser degree this is true of the traditions of all those world religions which have remained relevant throughout the ages in spite of great changes in the culture and circumstances of the lives of their adherents. This is one of the major differences between scientific theories and systems of religious belief.[32] In scientific theories, as Popper has correctly shown, falsifiability is a virtue. If a religious belief system is falsifiable, however, this merely goes to show that it is inadequate for the task of making sense of life and experience in *all* situations with which life could confront us. It is the task of theology to be innovative and to show how the belief system of a religious tradition can be creatively reinterpreted in ways which are both coherent and relevant to the changing demands of life.

5. Theology and Dialogue

This has profound implications for the ways in which theology tries to conceptualise the faith. Changes in the demands of life bring about changes in the aspects of faith which are relevant and necessary in order to make sense of life and cope meaningfully with our experience of the world. At different times and in different cultural situations, systematic theology therefore requires different conceptual models in order to highlight those aspects of the faith which are relevant to the cultural and historical situation and to filter out those aspects which are not relevant to the current demands of life. Sallie McFague provides a good example to illustrate this point:

> In an era when evil powers were understood to be palpable principalities in contest with God for control of human beings and the cosmos, the metaphor of Christ as the victorious king and lord, crushing the evil spirits and thereby freeing the world from their control, was indeed a powerful one. In our situation, however, to envision evil as separate from human beings rather than as the outcome of human decisions and actions, and to see the solution to evil as totally a divine responsibility, would be not only irrelevant to our time and its needs but harmful to them, for that would run counter to one of the central insights of the new sensibility: the need for human responsibility in a nuclear age.

In other words, in order to do theology, one must in each

> epoch do it differently. To refuse this task is to settle for a theology appropriate to some other time than one's own.[33]

Clearly, the task of theology is not merely descriptive, but innovative as well: it should not merely describe the conceptual grammar of a religious language-game, but should also develop innovative proposals which are both coherent and adequate to enable believers to cope with integrity with the changing demands of life.[34]

This also determines the agenda for a dialogue with non-believers about the tenability of theistic belief. We have tried to show the absurdity of construing this dialogue as a debate about the relative likelihood of there being a God. The endeavour of this kind of rational theology is absurd, necessarily fruitless and therefore irrational in the end. However, this rejection of rational theology does not entail a kind of fideism in which, as Kenny suggests, there can be no 'neutral rational grounds' to form the basis for a dialogue between believers and those outside the faith. We have shown that this dialogue is only meaningful if it is construed not as a debate about the likely truth of a proposition, but as a dialogue about the coherence and adequacy of the form of life which we could adopt with integrity. The question about the existence of God can only arise within the context of this debate. Atheists who reject the claim that theistic faith is coherent or adequate for coping with the demands of life, feel no need for the presupposition that God exists which is constitutive for this faith. It is up to them, therefore, to reflect on the form of life they could authentically adopt, and on the presuppositions which are constitutive of it. Christian theists, however, hold that the Christian faith can be coherently conceptualised in a form which is adequate for making sense of the demands with which life confronts them. If for this reason they can authentically make this form of life their own, then it is for them absurd to deny its constitutive proposition, namely that the God in whose sight they live and move and have their being, exists in reality.

Notes

1. Anthony Kenny, *The Five Ways* (London: 1968) 4.
2. Richard Swinburne, *The Coherence of Theism* (Oxford: 1977) 1.
3. Swinburne, *The Existence of God* (Oxford: 1977) 291.

4. See Karl Popper, *Conjectures and Refutations* (London: 1963) 33-41.
5. Ludwig Wittgenstein, *Philosophical Investigations*, ed. G.E.M. Anscombe and R. Rhees, trans. G.E.M. Anscombe (Oxford: 1953) I. 7. (References to Part I will be to the numbered remarks and to Part II to the pages).
6. *Investigations*, I, 23.
7. *Investigations*, II, 223.
8. George Pitcher, *The Philosophy of Wittgenstein* (Englewood Cliffs: 1965) 243.
9. Wittgenstein, *Lectures and Conversations on Aesthetics, Psychology and Religious Belief*, ed. Cyril Barrett (Oxford: 1966) 63, 71-72.
10. *Lectures on Religious Belief*, 71.
11. W.D. Hudson, 'Some remarks on Wittgenstein's account of religious belief', in G. N. A. Vesey, ed., *Talk of God* (London: 1969) 44.
12. For an illuminating treatment of this point, see Antony Flew, 'Freedom and human nature', *Philosophy* 66 (1991) 53-63. Flew criticises the rejection of this presupposition in the behaviourism of B. F. Skinner.
13. P.F. Strawson, *Individuals* (London: 1959) 35.
14. See Vincent Brümmer, *Theology and Philosophical Inquiry* (London: 1981) Chapter 2.
15. On this concept of 'necessity', see my *Theology and Philosophical Inquiry*, 283 - 290, and Chapter 4 of my *Speaking of a Personal God* (Cambridge: 1992).
16. J.N. Findlay, 'Can God's existence be disproved?', in A. Flew and A. MacIntyre, eds., *New Essays in Philosophical Theology* (London: 1955) 52.
17. Swinburne, *Existence of God*, 291.
18. See the reference to Strawson in note 13 above.
19. *Lectures on Religious Belief*, 59. See also 57.
20. W.D. Hudson, *Ludwig Wittgenstein. The Bearing of his Philosophy upon Religious Belief* (London: 1968) 56.
21. See D.Z. Phillips, 'Between faith and metaphysics', in Gijsbert van den Brink, Luco J. van den Brom & Marcel Sarot, eds., *Christian Faith and Philosophical Theology* (Kampen: 1992) 146-158.
22. For an extended analysis of ontological concepts like 'fact', 'exist', and 'real' which is more adequate in this context, see my *Theology and Philosophical Inquiry*, Chapters 17-19.
23. R.W. Hepburn, 'Poetry and religious belief', in A. MacIntyre,

Metaphysical Beliefs (London: 1957) 148.
24. For this term, see Chapter 7 of Janet Martin Soskice, *Metaphor and Religious Language* (Oxford: 1985).
25. On critical realism, see Chapter 3 of Ian Barbour, *Myths, Models and Paradigms* (London: 1974).
26. *Philosophical Investigations*, I, 23.
27. Wittgenstein, *Culture and Value* (Oxford: 1980) 27. In the *Philosophical Investigations* I, 23 Wittgenstein also compares the changes in language-games to changes in mathematics.
28. Kai Neilsen, 'Wittgensteinian Fideism', *Philosophy* 42 (1967) 119-209. See also Neilsen's *An Introduction to Philosophy of Religion* (London: 1982) Chapters 4-5.
29. Fergus Kerr mistakenly rejects 'the very idea that religion ... would count as a "form of life" in Wittgenstein's sense'. In this way he tries to avoid applying to religion the fideistic interpretation which he gives to this term in Wittgenstein. See Fergus Kerr, *Theology after Wittgenstein* (Oxford: 1986) 29.
30. See my *Theology and Philosophical Inquiry*, 61-63.
31. For this example see H.M. Kuitert, *Wat heet geloven?* (Baarn: 1977) 144-145.
32. For a more extended discussion of the differences between the language-games of science and religion, see Chapter 1 of Vincent Brümmer, ed., *Interpreting the Universe as Creation* (Kampen: 1991).
33. Sallie McFague, *Models of God* (London: 1987) 29-30.
34. Elsewhere I have defended this view of the task of theology more extensively. See Chapter 1 and the epilogue of *Speaking of A Personal God* (Cambridge: 1992), Chapter 1 of *The Model of Love* (Cambridge: 1993) and 'Philosophy, theology and the reading of texts' in *Religious Studies* 27 (1991) 451-462.

PART III

The Social Implications of the Christian Understanding of God

CHAPTER TEN

Some Reflections on the Social Doctrine of the Trinity

Jürgen Moltmann

I. The Trinitarian Understanding of the Unity of the Triune God

1. In the framework of the ancient metaphysics of substance, Tertullian formulated the unity of the triune God in a neuter and objective manner: *Una substantia = tres personae.* The unity of the three persons lies in their common divine substance. They are *homoousios.* They are one, but not one person. In the framework of the modern metaphysics of subject, Karl Barth and Karl Rahner identified the unity of the Trinity in a subjective and personal manner: one person in three modes of being, one subject in three distinct modes of subsistence. The unity of God's three modes of being lies in the one sovereign personality. God is one in three distinct modes of subsistence. In both ways of thinking, the unity of the triune God is not determined in a trinitarian but rather in a metaphysical manner, be it through the metaphysics of the cosmological proofs for the existence of God, according to which a deity is and the deity is one, or be it through the metaphysics of the transcendental subjectivity, according to which the deity is the self-willing and self-knowing subject and therefore must also be the subject of its own revelation and communication.

Both forms of thinking work from the assumption that the unity of the triune God precedes the threeness of the persons of God and is not formed through this. The starting point in both forms of thinking is the general metaphysics, not the special biblical salvation history. Therefore, the doctrines of the Trinity which are formed out of these two forms of thinking are also not useful as a hermeneutical key for the biblical witness of God. The doctrines of the Trinity which have been developed out of these metaphysical forms of thinking show clear tendencies towards modalism, such as in the neo-scholastic thesis of 'the one nature, the one knowledge and the one consciousness in God' which Barth and Rahner have taken up.

2. The Christian 'doctrine' of God arises out of the biblical 'history' of God, interprets it and leads into it. The Christian doctrine of the Trinity starts with the three distinct actors of this history: Father, Son and Holy Spirit, and asks about their unity. While Paul and the Synoptic Gospels mean the Father of Jesus Christ with 'God', we find a trinitarian language in the Gospel of John: 'I and the Father are one'; 'he who has seen me has seen the Father' because 'I am in the Father and the Father is in me' (Jn 14: 7-17). The Son and the Father are personally related to each other as I and Thou and through mutual indwelling form their unity which is expressed through the first person plural 'we' and 'us'. The divine persons exist in their mutual relationships for one another and through their reciprocal indwelling in each other. These intimate indwellings and complete, reciprocal interpenetrations are expressed by the term of the trinitarian *perichoresis.* This is the trinitarian understanding of unity because it combines threeness and oneness without reducing the threeness to the oneness or the oneness to the threeness and avoids the dangers of modalism as well of tritheism. If we understand the inner divine life perichoretically, then the divine life is fulfilled as little by one subject alone as by the trinitarian history of salvation. The unity of the triune God exists in the unity of the divine persons. The divine persons form through themselves a unique, incomparable and complete fellowship. The subjectivity of each one of them and their intersubjectivity are to be understood in a complementary manner, just as also the consciousness of each one of them and the will of each one of them and their common consciousness and their common will.

Because the salvation of the creation exists in being included in the eternal life of the triune God and in participating in it, we understand the unity of the triune God as an open, inviting, uniting and therefore integral community (Jn 17: 21: '...that they may also be in us'). If sin consists in the separation of the creatures from the source of their life, then salvation lies in their inclusion into the community of eternal life. This union with God is not only an external unity. It occurs in that the Holy Spirit takes the creatures into its community with the Son and the Father.

This community of creatures with God is also a perichoretic unity: 'He who abides in love abides in God, and God abides in him' (1 Jn 4: 16). The *perichoresis* is also the life secret of the new creation in which God will be 'all in all' (1 Cor 15: 28) and everything will be in God. The perichoretic unity of the triune God is therefore a social, an inviting, unifying and therefore world-open community: the community of the divine persons is open so wide that the whole world finds room within it.

II. The Trinitarian Understanding of the Divine Persons

1. The traditional term 'person' in the doctrine of the Trinity originates out of the ancient metaphysics of substance: '*Persona est rationalis naturae individua substantia*' (Boethius). As the new feminist theology has rightfully criticised, this definition reflects the separated self of the man which is indivisible and exists out of itself and which comes out of our Greco-Roman cultural history (Catherine Keller) and can therefore claim neither universal validity nor truth. The reduction of the three divine persons to the 'three modes of being' of the one sovereign divine subject originates out of the modern metaphysics of subjectivity. The rejection of the term 'person' through Barth and Rahner misses the modern understanding of the person because, in philosophy, the substantial and individualistic understanding of the person has been long ago replaced by a relational and social understanding of the person. The social trinitarian doctrine understands the divine person as a social self which is full of connections and capable of communication, and understands its subjectivity in its trinitarian intersubjectivity.

2. Person, relation and community are of the same origin because personality, relationality and sociality arise only with each other and at the same time. This means: 'Abba', the Father of Jesus Christ, is the Father of this Son. His Fatherhood in respect of this Son constitutes his person. He is neither the 'Father' *per se* as the Orthodox theology appears to think, nor in his person anything other than his 'Fatherhood' as Western theology has thought since Thomas when they say: '*Persona* is *relatio*'. The person does not precede the relationship, nor does the person dissolve in the relationship. Both are like the fellowship, arising at the same time. But because the relationships in the trinitarian fellowships of God are different, the personalities are therefore also different. The use of one and the same term 'person' (or that which is put in its place) for the Father, the Son and the Holy Spirit blurs their

concrete differences and the unique characteristics and is the first step towards modalism. If one wants to remain concrete, then one must form unique personal terms for each, that is for the Father, for the Son and for the Holy Spirit. General terms expose only the common points, not the unique ones. But in the original relationships of the Trinity, everything is unique because it occurs for the first time.

From the beginning there were two metaphors for the mystery of the divine Trinity: the one originates from the Christ story and speaks of Father-Son-Holy Spirit, the other originates from the creation story and speaks of God-Word-Breath. Some problems of the doctrine of the Trinity arise out of the unwitting intermixing of the two metaphors. If one understands them as mutual complements, then each person of the Trinity has two names: the first person is Father and Speaker, the second person Son and Word, the third person Spirit and Breath.

a). *God the Father* is in the Christian faith always the 'Abba' of Jesus Christ, that is, the Father of this Son, never the Father of all things, Zeus, nor the Father of the Gods, Jupiter, in whose name Jesus was crucified. Only after the Constantinian 'turn' were the two father figures fused (Lactantius) and the Father of Jesus Christ was abused as God of the Christian Caesars and of patriarchy. Only from Jesus is God to be called 'Father': 'Whoever sees me sees the Father.' Otherwise no one sees him. As soon as one calls God 'Father', the Son is present. The relationship of the Father to this Son is therefore identified as 'begotten' (Ps 2:7) as well as 'birth'. According to the Council of Toledo (675), the Son came *de utero Patris.* As in Jesus' own Abba-secret, it has to do with a motherly father or a fatherly mother, in any case, about the name for the original trust in the eternal love. The eternal birthing and creative love is therefore ascribed to the Father. He is not *individua substantia*, but rather the communicating self which lives in his relationships. The Father loves the Son with productive love and exists by virtue of this love not in himself but rather totally in the Son. He gives himself up totally in the Son. He gives himself up totally to the Son.

b). *God the Son* is the child of God's eternal love of the motherly Father. The Father loves the Son with productive love, the Son loves the Father with responding love. Just as the Father is totally in the Son, so the Son is totally in the Father and not in himself. The productive and the responding love do not exist in balanced mutuality. Therefore the productive love of the Father is open for further responses by creatures which correspond to the Son and fulfil the joy of the Father. Out of the productive love of the Father for the eternal child arises creative love. Creation arises out of the Father's love of the Son and is intended to harmonise with the Son's responsive love. The creation is the gift of the Father to the Son and her redemption is the Son's gift to the Father. The Son is born from the Father through the Spirit, because the birth of the Son is accompanied by the Spirit coming forth from the Father. Just as the Spirit is nothing without the Son, so the Son is nothing without the Spirit. This makes the word-metaphor for the Son clear: God speaks his eternal word in the breath of his eternal Spirit. Only the *filioque* of the Western church prohibits this thought. If one takes both metaphors together, one must then say: the Son arises out of the Father and the Spirit, just as the Spirit arises out of the Father and the Son.

c). According to the Nicene Creed, *God the Spirit* arises 'out of the Father.' That can only mean: it arises out of the Father of the Son and has its origin in the Father's relationship to the Son. It arises out of the Fatherhood of the Father and therefore cannot be thought of without the Sonship of the Son. The Son is present and involved with the Father in the coming forth of the Spirit. He 'accompanies' the coming forth of the Spirit out of the Father like the word accompanies the breath. The Spirit which arises at the same time with the Son from the Father, rests upon the Son. The Son becomes the recipient and the residence of the Spirit. The Spirit which rests upon the Son shines forth from the Son and brings the eternal light into the eternal love and the eternal life of the triune God. Just as love is primarily ascribed to the Father and grace to the Son, so is fellowship ascribed to the Spirit (2 Cor 13:13).

The Spirit is not the fellowship of the Father and of the Son. The *vinculum amoris* already exists in the reciprocity of their mutual love. It exists, however, in its fellowship with the Father and the Son. The Spirit makes the perichoretic fellowship of the Trinity arise from the reciprocal relationship of the Father and the Son. Therefore, the Spirit is also experienced by humans as 'the Godhead with fellowship characteristics' (Friedrich Hölderlin) or as 'Go-Between God' (John Taylor). Because Spirit experience is most of all fellowship experience, the personality of the Holy Spirit must be described differently from the personality of the Father and that of the Son. While with the Father, the vis-a-vis (Gegenüber) is perceived, with the Holy Spirit the present (Gegenwart) is experienced. If we live 'in the Holy Spirit' then the Spirit is not discernible as the vis-a-vis, as little as we see the eye with which we see or recognise the standpoint on which we stand. From this we conclude that it belongs to the character of the Spirit to be a vis-a-vis in an encompassing presence just as the Mother is at first an encompassing presence to the child before she is perceived by the child as a personal vis-a-vis. The often mentioned 'anonymity' of God the Spirit comes from this, God's special personality which can not at all be understood as *individua substantia*. It is not indivisible but rather capable of communication; it is not *substantia* which is separated from all relationships but rather a fellowship-being capable of relationships; it does not present the rational nature but rather the encompassing divine life.

III. The Trinitarian Understanding of the Likeness of God

1. Since Augustine, Western church theology has used the psychological analogy in order to interpret the human's likeness to God in a trinitarian manner. According to the 'psychological doctrine of the Trinity' (Michael Schmaus), the human's *imago Dei* lies in their (asexual) *natura intellectualis*, while their bodies, like all other bodily things, show only *vestigia Dei*. The *imago Dei* is imprinted into every reasonable soul: 'Because in the uncreated Trinity there are differences based on the coming forth of the Word from the speaking one and the coming forth of the Word from both, one can speak of an image of the uncreated Trinity in the case of the creature which is gifted with reason and in which is found a coming forth of the Word in the intellect and the coming forth of the love in the will' (Thomas Aquinas, *Summa Theologiae* 1.a. q. 93 art. 6).

As subject of intellect and will, each soul is a likeness of the Trinity: being corresponds to the Father, knowledge to the Son, love to the Spirit. As subject of intellect and will, each soul corresponds to God the Father. Each soul dominates the body: *anima forma corporis*. Just as the soul dominates the body and is its head, so must the man dominate the woman, Christ the man, and God Christ (1 Cor 11). 'The man is origin and goal of the woman, just as God is origin and goal of the entire creation' (Thomas Aquinas, *Summa Theologica* 1. a. q. 93 art. 4). But according to the biblical tradition, God created the humans to a likeness, 'as man and woman he created them' (Gen 1: 26-28). God's likeness holistically determines the soul and body of the humans, male and female, and determines the human socially. As a result of this the trinitarian understanding of God's likeness must also be social. Not each divided and isolated soul alone, but rather humans in their holistic fellowship are the likeness of the triune God. Just as the Father, Son and Spirit form a unique, incomparable fellowship in the *perichoresis,* humans become *imago Trinitatis* in the fellowship of love, of friendship and of the Holy Spirit. Anthropologically, this does not mean the I-Thou relationship nor the family, but rather the fundamental *anthropological triangle* which is a result of the unity and generativity of the humans: each human person is man or woman, and their parents' child. The man-woman relationship denotes the sociality of the humans, the parent-child relationship the generativity. The first is the sexual fellowship in space, the second is the fellowship of the generations in time. If the whole person is meant to be *imago Trinitatis,* then with this the human fellowship is meant.

The inner-trinitarian *perichoresis* is archetype and model for this type of God-corresponding fellowship. Father, Son and Spirit have everything in common except for their personal characteristics. They do not exist with each other, but rather empty themselves on to each other and live in each other by virtue of love. This kinetic and perichoretic fellowship is also the life-principle of the creation which reflects God's glory. It is also the experience of the fellowship of the Holy Spirit in Christ's community, as Acts 4:3ff reports: they 'were of one heart and soul; they had everything in common; there was not a needy person among them; distribution was made to each as any had need.' When the church is such an 'icon of the Trinity', she can also become a life-principle of human society: a society without privileges – a society without poverty and need – a society of free and equal persons. Then the Trinity will become our 'social programme', the program of social personalism, or of personal Socialism. We would overcome the possessive individualism of the West as well as the depersonalising collectivism of the East. We would be able to integrate a human 'culture of sharing' symbiotically into the perichoretic texture of nature and to live and become blessed together with the fellowship of the entire creation in the fellowship of the triune God.

CHAPTER ELEVEN

The Christian Rhetoric of God and Human Relational Experience

Janet Martin Soskice

Professor Freyne (See Chapter 3) has pointed out that the difference between the early Christians and other Jews was not over monotheism but rather with how the Christian belief in a crucified Redeemer could be interpreted, and what the social implications of that might be. I should like to recall as well Dr Schwöbel's point that trinitarian language was not developed to reject the Jewish heritage but rather to enable Christians to retain and stand within it. Already we can see developing a problem that is ours but which has been the problem of every generation of Christian theologians. It is that our formulations which attempt to do one thing can be read as doing another, for instance, we speak of 'triunity' but it can look like tritheism. Thus, in classical expositions or in modern ones like that of Walter Kasper, we find talk about the absolute unity of God *despite* the distinction of persons, and the absolute equality of the persons *despite* the dependence of the second person on the first and the third on the first and the second, and so on.[1] To many people in the pews, and not just to them, this kind of 'despite' language sounds a little like Orwell's *Animal Farm* – 'all animals are equal but some animals are more equal than others'. Similarly, trinitarian language may be intended as a corrective to idolatry, the worship of more than the one God, but how successful is it? I take this point to be part of what Dr Loades meant when she reminded us how frequently one hears phrases like 'divine fatherhood does not have masculine characteristics but… ' Like most people, Christians are very good at rejecting heresies they never found attractive anyway (like tritheism) and pretty good at retaining, under the guise of orthodoxy, heresies they really quite like, such as various types of subordinationism, monarchianism, and celestial sexism – all in their own way idolatrous. We cannot in this century be innocent of the fact that theological formulations, while defensible and even worthy at the level of theory – the level at which we as professional theologians work – have their ideological deployments too. We cannot either doubt or brush this aside, as maybe earlier generations (pre-nineteenth century theologians) might. After Foucault and Ricoeur, no one can be so innocent. To give an example: at the level of pure theological theory God is 'I am who I am', Creator and not creature, and *a fortiori* not a male creature; at the level of ideology God has been styled as male in the Jewish and Christian religions. God has been styled as 'Father', for instance. Nothing necessarily is wrong with that in itself, but we should be aware that this stylisation has been read in particular ways, certain views of what fathers are and should be, of what rights fathers have and so on, have been read onto it, and the 'rights' of fatherhood have in turn been used to underwrite patterns of dominance in families, between married partners, between states and so on, in ways that have not always been admirable.

So what do we do? Do we remove the metaphors? Do we cease to tell stories? Or do we work from more lively awareness of our necessarily modest metaphors and necessarily partial tale-telling in our attempts to speak of God? I worry about purging the tales because history aptly illustrates that by purging metaphors and stories one does not end up with a theology that is scientific and free of fable, but, on the contrary, with a theology which takes *a* particular fable, probably a very metaphysical, abstract and sophisticated one, as the straightforward account of how things are 'chez God'. Furthermore, purgers seem to assume that symbols are stable, that symbols are born evil and remain evil. But symbols aren't stable. If they were, they would probably be idols and certainly need to be challenged. Take one of the central ones, already mentioned – calling God 'Father'. Paul Ricoeur has argued that, far from being a stable symbol in the texts of the Judaeo-Christian tradition, this is highly mobile, incomplete, diverse and variable according to its placing in the Biblical texts.[2] He notes (and it is certainly noteworthy) that the divine title 'Father' is scarcely used in the texts of the Hebrew bible. God is represented as 'father' only eleven times in the Old Testament, and never invoked in prayed by this title, whereas Jesus calls God 'Father' over one hundred and seventy times in the Gospels and never invokes God in prayer by any other title. From this information Ricoeur, using the freedom that a philosopher and literary critic has, tells a new tale. He says that Jesus, in calling God 'Father', announces a new time. In Ricoeur's terms it is the arrival of children that makes someone father. It is not the father who makes children; rather, the coming of children makes someone a father since 'father' is, semantically, a dependent title. So, Ricoeur says, its only with Jesus, as the first born among the children of God, that God becomes Father and is named 'Father' in the distinctive sense. So, the coming of the Son, in a sense, gives birth to the Father. Continuing the Christian narrative, it is in the Son's death that the distinct nature of divine fatherhood is established, for the death of the Son is in some sense also the death of the Father, who is one with the Son. I found a parallel to this suggestive idea of Ricoeur's in an unexpected source, the book of the French philosopher Julia Kristeva, *In the Beginning was Love.*[3] This is one of a series of books in which psychoanalysts explain what they understand the psychoanalytic task to be. A Lacanian (of a sort) and a French feminist (of a sort), Kristeva begins her discussion with Freud's observation that the foundation of his cure is 'Our God Logos'. She describes her own perception of the psychoanalytic task as one of making word and flesh meet, of making the word become flesh in the discourse of love. She is writing as (as far as we know) an agnostic, yet she develops her comments by an analysis of the Apostles' Creed. She notes that, in the Genesis narratives, God is represented as creating by separating. Separation is the mark of God's presence – the separation of light and dark, sea and dry land, male and female, and this dividing and separating reaches a climax in the Christian story of the crucifixion, with the abandonment of Christ on the cross and the cry of dereliction. To add my own theological gloss to this: as she represents it, the supreme moment of *creation* is the 'separation' of God from God – the cry of dereliction. Yet, Kristeva continues, it is because one is deserted, in psychoanalytic terms, that one may achieve ecstasy and completion, and the union with the father who, she adds, is 'himself a substitution for the mother'. (In psychoanalytic terms it is the mother with whom we all seek that final, primary union). If her reading is correct, then the symbolic weight of this Christian narrative concerns a fusion with the Other who is both mother and father. Now we could say, bringing the stories of Ricoeur and Kristeva together, that the death of the Son and of the Father who is one with the Son, make possible a new birth, the *ekstasis* which is the mission of the Spirit. It is through this Spirit (often styled in the tradition as feminine) that the Son is raised to new life, reborn. The trinitarian narrative is thus reversed – the Son is dependent on the Spirit, and the Father is dependent in turn on the Son, because it is children who make someone a father. The Father in this story can no longer, at least at a symbolic level, have the divine property of innascibility (the attribute of being independent of birth) which has been prized by some trinitarian theologians but associated only with the Fatherhood of God. In this story the Father too 'is born' of the Son and of the Spirit. God dies and God is born. Isn't something of this what the trinitarian formulations have wanted to catch? What then does this tell us of human, relational experience? I would suggest that we do not need a doctrine of the Trinity to teach us how to be relational beings, or what it is to be relational. In fact something is gone very seriously wrong if we ask that kind of question. Walter Kasper draws the following contrast between God and us. He says that whereas God *is* relational, we humans only *choose* to be relational. He adds, 'relations are essential only to the full self-realisation of the being. A human being is, and remains a human being, even if he selfishly closes himself against relations with others'. Surely this is untrue. We need other human beings, notably parents, to come into being at all! *Which* human being is free of human relations – name the person who didn't have any parents? As infants we are entirely dependent on others for our existence. Those others teach us language, values, stories, – in short – a world. Even our limited capacity to 'close ourselves off from others', is only conceivable because we have already been socially constituted. I need other people even in order to shut myself off from them. This kind of argument is the thrust of Charles Taylor's book *Sources of the Self*.[4] We are constituted as selves, not despite others, but because of and by others. The more we are 'in relation' the more we *are* our selves. Alison Jaggar points out that modern western political philosophy has been dominated by the Hobbesian problem: how is co-operation between men possible? But if philosophers had taken heed of the actual processes of human reproduction and childrearing, the vast amount of adult co-operation necessary to bring even one child to independent adulthood, the better question might have been: where does ethical egoism come from?[5] We are relational beings and if this isn't obvious to us it only shows how deeply we are prey to one of the most insidious of myths or fairy stories, the myth of the Cartesian *cogito*, the atomistic and entirely free, fictional agent of modern philosophy. This is the hero of the texts of the Enlightenment, as Iris Murdoch has pointed out – free, rational, independent, responsible and detached. Charles Taylor calls this figment 'disengaged man'. The exclusive language is deliberate, for this is a masculine man; the new agent of the new seventeenth century science who gains control, even in his moral life – by disengagement and objectification, even to the extent of objectifying himself. But his Cartesian *cogito*, this atomistic agent, has been, I think, decisively vanquished years ago. We can point to this as a philosophical achievement. Wittgenstein has shown him to be epistemologically threadbare; Charles Taylor shows him to be morally bankrupt; Foucault shows him to be a social and scientific nonsense; Lacan and Irigaray show him to be psychologically pathological! Is it surprising that this period, from the sixteenth to the twentieth century has been, as Lacan has said, the 'ego's era'? Is it surprising that the same period during which deism has triumphed and trinitarian orthodoxy partially eclipsed is one which has seen a constant decline in religious practice in western Europe? Is it coincidence that a favoured picture of God in this period has been, as Gabriel Daly points out, Newton's absentee landlord? Modern Man, with his overweening desire for certainty and control, makes a 'god' who underwrites his certainty, an unmysterious God who is easily controlled, a deist 'god' who is in the back room playing billiards until he winds everything up. As Kasper points out (to invoke him this time on the side of the righteous), the title of the deist writer Toland's book is highly significant – *Christianity not Mysterious*. A God who is no longer mystery generates human persons who are no longer mystery. They too are objects that can be manipulated in a world of manipulable objects. Kristeva suggests that psychoanalysis is perhaps the final length of objectification where even the subconscious life becomes an 'object' of scientific analysis. So, we get this postmodernist trajectory: the death of God leads to the death of man (the human subject) leads to the death of value, the death of meaning, of meanings in texts and so on.

My hope is that, if these last four hundred years has been a period of 'the absentee God', and non-theologies, that the next four hundred years in the life of Trinity College, Dublin might see a renaissance. Not just Christianity but the whole of western culture needs a fresh understanding here. What I like about trinitarian theology and why I want to insist that it is not, despite many scholarly obituaries, dead, is that it seems to me a language of God Here Now. That's very simple. If it did a piece of work in the first Christian centuries, it is likely to have a piece of work to do today; not to tell us about ourselves (we always want more on that topic) but to tell us about what God is, and what it is that God can be. The students of theology that I meet are, characteristically, sub-trinitarian even if they are good, even biblical Christians. They tend to believe in a Christ who is a demi-God or a semi-God, some kind of a divine messenger. God (in this account) is up there in the back of beyond and sends someone to tell us how to get right with him. But as trinitarian Christians we should insist that in the incarnation we meet true God. We do not meet a messenger boy. In Jesus we meet true God. The telling of trinitarian stories must be of continual importance for preserving this truth, and it's also partly what the doctrine of the Trintiy is about. Augustine, as a young man, was appalled by the barbarity of Christianity as compared with the more sophisticated Greco-Roman religions then on offer. He found especially distasteful all the stories in the Hebrew bible of those peoples with their horrible polytheism and immoral marital behaviour. But when he fully embraced Christianity (some time after he saw the intellectual persuasiveness of its neo-Platonic apologists), he seemed to see how important it was in the Jewish and Christian narratives that God has a human history. That is what the doctrine of the incarnation insists upon. And once Augustine believed God could have a human history, then the human history of the Jews, warts and all, became not simply a distraction to the story of 'God with us' but the very place where God is revealed. Augustine could then see that his own human history was also the place of God's divine disclosure: he could write the *Confessions*. By implication each life and every human history is a place where God is known: God here, now, past, present and to be. It seems to me that trinitarian formulations at their best protect this presence of God Here Now, with you, with me, with the grandest philosopher and the most modest slave girl of the second century. This legacy of God Here Now, in everyone's story, totally present, is a precious legacy. I'd like to hang on to it, and use the trinitarian language to do so.

Notes

1. Walter Kasper, *The God of Jesus Christ* (London: SCM Press, 1983) 268-9.
2. Paul Ricoeur, 'Fatherhood: from phantasm to symbol' in D. Ihde, ed., *The Conflict of Interpretations* (Evanston: Northwestern University Press, 1974) 468. I discuss Ricoeur's article at length in my essay, 'Can a Feminist Call God "Father"?' in Teresa Elwer, ed., *Women's Voices* (London: Marshall Pickering, 1992).
3. *In the Beginning was Love: Psychoanalysis and Faith* (New York: Columbia University Press, 1987).
4. *Sources of the Self* (Cambridge: CUP, 1989).
5. *Feminist Politics and Human Nature* (London: Harvest Press, 1983).

CHAPTER TWELVE

Some Elementary Remarks on the Word 'God'

James M. Byrne

> The Word 'God' signifies the divine nature: it is used to mean something that is above all that is, and that is the source of all things and is distinct from them all. That is how those that use it mean it to be used. (*Thomas Aquinas*)

> As far as I am concerned, what I see in religion is not the mystery of the incarnation but the mystery of the social order: it prevents the rich from being massacred by the poor by relegating the idea of equality to heaven. (*Napoleon Bonaparte*)

> Social life is essentially practical. All mysteries which mislead theory into mysticism find their rational solution in human practice and in the comprehension of this practice. (*Karl Marx*)[1]

The papers delivered to this historic colloquium attest to the richness and diversity of several thousand years of reflection on the nature and experience of the deity. Their own richness and diversity also point to the burden which modern theology has to bear in thinking about God, confronted as it is on the one hand with the attempt to find some firm way of creatively analysing the meaning and aim of religion in a world of increasing complexity, and on the other hand with an explosion of cultural and historical sources which make that task more interesting, but also much more difficult.

In a world of increasing theological complexity, it might be profitable, I think, to attempt simply to think through, however briefly, some implications of considering the word 'God' as theologically and culturally problematic, that is, as a word which is a question and a problem to itself. As we will see, considering this word in itself leads us beyond the mere word to the world that is the context and the home of this word. In particular, I would like to pay attention to the word 'God' as a theological symbol with important ethical bearing. My remarks will be in the context of the Christian view of God, although I believe that they are not insignificant for other religions.

Is this word 'God' a dead word, as Nietzsche so famously claimed? Is it a word whose meaning has become so arbitrary that it is no longer possible to give it any real content outside the limits of theological discourse? Is it a word, like its close associate in the Christian tradition, 'love', that has been so battered by its popular uses and misuses that it at once means both everything and nothing? Is it a word of intimacy (*Abba*) which has been peddled in the backstreets of language until its faded glory merits not a glance from the casual passer-by? These questions are partly rhetorical and perhaps unanswerable. But at least we must attempt to formulate the problem as accurately as possible. I shall begin to explore the question of this word by reference to two very different thinkers, Nietzsche and Rahner.

When, in Nietzsche's *The Gay Science*, the madman staggers into the bright morning light, foolishly carrying a lit lantern, we are witnessing undoubtedly one of the pivotal moments in the religious experience of the West. What is all too often forgotten, in the context of the conventional reading of Nietzsche as virulently anti-religious, is that the madman is *searching for God*. He is not one of the smug burghers who joke of God's fear of them, and ask if perhaps God has gone away. Nietzsche, more than the complacent Christianity and self-sufficient atheism of his day, realised acutely the consequences of the absence of God. Has not the universe grown colder?; have we not unchained ourselves from the sun that was the centre of all?; have we not destroyed all hope of purity, of salvation, by abandoning the ultimate symbol to which we could cling in the hope of fulfillment? As we know from Nietzsche's other writings, the death of God is an event of language; but this does not mean that it is merely a linguistic event. 'The death of God' is not simply the death of a word which will decay and disappear from use, as Marx thought, but it is primarily the death of a system of values and beliefs which were crystallised in this one word. The 'death of God' marks the disappearance of that complex political, religious, cultural and economic system that was Christendom. Strangely, and again counter to many interpretations of the rise of atheism, this disappearance of the world which revolved around 'God'– the world of Augustine, Abelard, Dante, Catherine of Siena, the Gothic cathedral and the great religious wars – is not *caused* by our becoming gods in the place of the one God, for – according to Nietzsche – this is an event which is still to come (the advent of the *Übermensch* was, alas, a more sordid affair than Nietzsche would have hoped). What then is at the kernel of the dissipation of the symbolic world that had God at its centre?

Nietzsche's madman offers no clear answer to this question. However, in our time the most dominant academic answer has been offered by post-structuralist critics and philosophers who have drawn on the Nietzschean heritage: the death of God is an event in language, which empties the word God of all possible content and meaning because no linguistic construct can capture reality through reference; all words are defined, as Saussure pointed out, 'horizontally' in relation to other words and not 'vertically' in relation to things (or gods). Language does not give us access to 'reality'; religious language has no reference beyond itself. Now this is indeed the modern problematic of epistemological skepticism (to be found also in more virulent form in the logical positivism which came from the Vienna Circle), but when stripped of its deconstructionist rhetoric, it is seen to be little more than Kant's critique of metaphysical theology – that we cannot speculate metaphysically beyond the bounds of experience – applied to language, a critique which gave rise to modern theology (primarily through Schleiermacher's reaction to Kant) and its attempt to locate the content of the word 'God' in the innermost experience of the person.

According to Karl Rahner, one of the most influential advocates of a theology of experience in this century, the word 'God' as such has no 'content'; it is nameless, faceless and silent.[2] Its content must come from elsewhere. But where is this elsewhere? In the Christian tradition, at least, this 'elsewhere' is primarily, but not exclusively, the life and witness of Jesus of Nazareth. It is from the life, death and resurrection of Jesus that we can know who God is. Yet this one life, the tradition of the race which preceded it and the tradition of the church which follows it do not give us a univocal answer to the question of content. Instead there are many answers, thus giving rise to the issue of the relevant importance of the various texts, doctrines, authorities and experiences. As Marcion perceived clearly, the question of God and the question of canonicity are forever intertwined.

But the 'canon', whatever its content, is not the only possible source of knowledge of God. Is it possible, as Rahner believed, that some knowledge of the content of this mysterious word 'God' is given at the point of depth experience in which 'theology and anthropology become one'?[3] Furthermore, is it in face to face encounter with the very word 'God' that something of the unthematic content, the 'reality' of the word is given to us? Can this very word keep open the possibilities for being human to such an extent that with its disappearance it would be the case 'that man himself had died' ?[4]

It is at this point, where theology and anthropology meet, that we see an uncanny problematic shared by Rahner and Nietzsche. Is God acting in us or do we become gods? Is the transcendentality of experience an openness to the transcendent deity or to the possibilities of becoming an *Übermensch*? The duplicity of experience matches that of language. Is it any wonder that the mystics, like Descartes, sometimes doubted whether they were hearing the voice of God or that of the devil?

While it is not so strange that the transcendental analysis of experience – so prevalent in nineteenth century Protestant theology after Schleiermacher and developed in Roman Catholic theology in the twentieth century by Rahner, Lonergan and others – could be interpreted as collapsing the divine into the human, as Barth asserted so strongly, this is not the only major point at issue. For the correspondence between the duplicity of experience and that of language raises immediately the most important question, that of ethics. The ethical question arises inescapably because language not only *precedes* our reflection on the world, as Derrida and others constantly remind us, it also *provokes and permeates* our action in it. This is particularly true of the word 'God', whose content, if it can be established to any degree, gives not merely speculative insight into onto-theology, but is also expected to tell us something about how life should be lived.

Classically – as in Augustine and those, like Luther, who followed him – the ethical import of the word 'God' was configured in terms of will. To behave ethically was to follow the will of God, which, even in Protestantism, was usually channeled to the believer through the mediation of church leaders. The emphasis on the will of God and obedience to it creates the permanent temptation of religion to dogmatism and intolerance through the repressed consciousness of the fragility of the word 'God': God's will can be known through revelation; as it is known it must be followed; and as it can be followed it must be followed absolutely. Dogmatism turns its face from the wound of language and experience, ignores the alienation at the heart of the human, and spurns the homelessness of the religious consciousness, whose 'essence is the search for lost intimacy'[5] (Georges Bataille). In so doing it denies the word 'God' as question and closes itself to the possibility of transcending the finite, the very mark of religious experience.

So this 'almost ridiculously exhausting and demanding word' (Rahner),[6] 'God', must be given content, a content that includes the ethical (otherwise it is useless as regards our actual lives) but that results neither in submission to divine will as interpreted by the few nor, if the word is to retain its original independence, in a Nietzschean identification of the divine will with the human will to power and domination.

Outside the safe haven of a Barthian confidence in the certainty of revelation, it is a difficult task for theology to discern what this word contains – or, if one prefers, what it means, signifies, portrays, reveals, etc. The difficulty of this task is accentuated by a contemporary pessimism regarding the ability of diverse cultural, ideological, historical and theological consciousnesses to reach some form of commensurability. To put this at its most straightforwardly theological, how can one theology of the one God (even if such a thing were possible) fulfil the requirement of David Tracy and others to reach the different 'publics' of academy, church and wider society? When it is acknowledged that each of these 'publics' has myriad subdivisions with countless views of what 'God' is and means, the task of achieving some form of common agreement would appear impossible.[7]

To take just one obvious but nonetheless apposite example: the different uses and concepts of God employed by two of the most vibrant, yet opposed movements in Christianity today, namely American evangelical fundamentalism and liberation/feminist theology. Contemporary fundamentalism utilises a notion of God which is derived from a literal interpretation of scripture and which is employed to distinguish the adherents of this God from the rest of the (sinful) society. It aims to bring the laws and ethos of that society into line with the will of God as expressed through the Scriptures (a will which all too often appears to mirror the views of white, heterosexual, right-wing Americans). One of the ironies of this growth in fundamentalism is that – as Harvey Cox has accurately pointed out – it has its roots partly in a reaction to the historical-critical method of biblical interpretation, which had the effect of taking control of the Bible from lay people and giving into the possession of scholars; thus 'fundamentalism arose as a way of reclaiming the authority and accessibility of the Bible from the "modernists"'.[8] Even a passing knowledge of nineteenth century American evangelist religion enables one to see the parallels between this form of populist Christianity and contemporary fundamentalism.

The fundamentalist notion of God rejects the achievements of academic theology, is sectarian in its ecclesiology and aggressive in its stance towards contemporary liberal society. In this respect, fundamentalism continues the classical tradition's relation of the word 'God' to concrete ethical reality through the notion of 'God's will', but with results rather similar to many abuses of the past. One of the upshots of this, as Cox observes, is that modern theology's hope that in luring the intellectual elite back to religion, the 'plebeians' would follow, has badly misfired. The 'plebeians' have gone their own way.

Liberation theology, in contrast, particularly in Latin America, has both attempted to hold firm to modern critical methods of theology and to allow the voice of popular piety to be heard, hoping that each could inform the other. This has not been without its difficulties,[9] but it has given us a vision of God much more in keeping with the freedom, dignity and equality of human beings irrespective of economic standing, race or gender difference.

It is clear that the enormous differences in the social, economic and sexual politics of these two opposing strands of Christianity are due to a great extent to their differing views of God. This, in turn, can be traced, but is not reducible to, differing interpretations and uses of scripture, history, philosophy, social studies, etc. Now, as regards offering a response to the fundamentalist viewpoint, I believe that it is too facile to think that academic theology can of itself retrieve the idea of God from the fundamentalists, for it is the modern theological endeavour, as Cox has pointed out, which has contributed to some degree to the growth of this phenomenon, and it is its very methods which are rejected by fundamentalism.

What is at stake in the modern problematic of 'God' is indeed the meaning of this word, but what this example serves to show is that the meaning of the word 'God' – and therefore its retrieval – cannot be separated from the ethical (and this means social, political, economic, sexual and environmental) history of this word. In other words, what is at stake is not simply the theological history of the word, but rather the *ethical history of mainstream Christianity itself.* For it is in the ethical history of Christianity that the word 'God' finds its true content and it can only be retrieved from fundamentalists or from a fragmentary form of popular pluralism by reinvesting it with something of its meaning as a word of intimacy, compassion, justice and hope. This can only happen through action informed by a critical theology which itself is informed by experience (this is what I take to be the meaning of *praxis*).

It is my belief therefore – and in this I am in close agreement with many feminist and liberation theologians – that the past and future meaning of the word 'God' is inextricably bound up with the way in which the symbols, traditions, authorities, political structures, gender roles, etc. of the religious tradition (and this means essentially the people who profess belief in 'God') function in the world in concrete situations.[10] I am also in agreement with George Lindbeck's claim that religious language can only begin to be called ontologically 'true' when that language first forms part of a coherent pattern of speech and action which reflects the values that are contained within the religious system as a whole – Lindbeck's provocative example is that of a crusader who does not remain within the totality of Christian belief when he cleaves the skull of the infidel with the cry *'Christus est Dominus'*.[11] Without this contextual and ethical coherence, religious truth-claims (e.g. for the 'goodness' of God) can appear paradoxical and meaningless: as Lindbeck puts it, this contextual (or, 'intrasystemic') truth is 'a necessary but not sufficient condition for ontological truth'.[12] One could also follow J.L. Austin here: religious utterances can be considered ontologically true only when they are considered 'performative utterances', that is, when they make present to some degree the reality they attempt to depict.[13]

It could be objected that this view fails to distinguish between the goodness of God and the sinfulness of the believer. However, when this 'sinfulness' is not reducible to individual instances, when it becomes systematic and endemic to religious institutions or practices, then the veracity of the whole belief-system is called into question. This is the point made forcibly by, for example, feminist theologians' critique of ecclesial patriarchy and the theological justification often given for it.

This assertion of the necessity of the ethical or 'performative' condition for the truth of religious language raises the question as to why modern Western theology, in its analysis of the massive popular rejection of religion which characterises the West – a rejection which has its roots to a great extent in the identification of God with structures of injustice and oppression – has chosen to respond primarily with intellectual arguments on the question of the existence of God, rather than with an analysis of the possible religious causes of that rejection. Perhaps this has something to do with the Western philosophical and theological tradition's emphasis on the oneness of God and the unity of doctrine, thus blinding it to the manifestly diverse notions of God operating in different religious, socio-economic, and socio-sexual environments, as evidenced by the acute differences between the political values of evangelical fundamentalism and liberation/feminist theology. However, what is clear is that both liberation theology and evangelical fundamentalism (and also, of course, modern liberal theology) have underestimated the links between atheism and perverse images of God stemming from the perceived unethical behaviour of God's representatives, the one seeing atheism primarily as a European 'intellectual' problem which filtered down into the general population (unlike in South America) and the other as a secular plot to destroy religion.

Ultimately, then, an appelation such as 'Father, Son, and Holy Spirit' is not in itself the content or meaning of the word 'God' in the Christian tradition – no more than is 'Unmoved Mover', 'Abba', 'Cloud of Unknowing' or any other metaphorical language. These venerable terms only become meaningful, and begin to approximate something of the mysterious presence and absence of God in the Christian tradition, when the reality which they attempt to signify for us – human life as created, meaningful and capable of fulfillment as far as is possible – is made a reality in the smallest of ways. It is only a critically uninformed tradition such as existed for most of the first eighteen hundred years of Christianity, or an idealist tradition which gives the word 'God' a metaphysical status divorced from any basis in life, that could demand respect for a word by invoking the power of the word itself. One of the difficulties for modern theology in dealing with the use and abuse of the word 'God' has been the fact that when a critical theology did emerge on the back of the Enlightenment it did so in an idealist form. When the word 'God' (or other religious language) is used as if its meaning and reality is self-evident, or can be established speculatively, it is no more than a talisman (here, of course, Hegel is the great witch-doctor), and theology moves further away from its particular social, economic, political and ecclesial context. Rahner's statement quoted above that man would disappear with the word 'God' betrays the talismanic tendencies of the idealist metaphysics which has dominated modern theology, for if this word, as it has been for so long, is a symbol of oppression, then its disappearance would be the liberation of 'man' . This, of course, was the view of Marx, who thought that with the advent of the dictatorship of the proletariat the word 'God' would be no more. His faith in prophecy and dialectical materialism may now seem naive, but his formulation of the difficulty for the future career of 'God' was astute. For if the word does not represent and evoke justice, dignity, equality, and hope – the very best that this word represents in the Christian, and other, religious traditions – then its disappearance would not be lamented.

Notes

1. The quotations are from the following sources: Thomas Aquinas, *Summa Theologiae,* 1a, 13, 5; Napoleon Bonaparte, in Adrien Dansette, ed., *Napoléon, pensées politiques et sociales* (Paris: Flammarion, 1969) 146, quoted in Georges Casalis, *Correct Ideas Don't Fall from the Skies* (Maryknoll: Orbis, 1984) 40; and, Karl Marx, *Theses on Feuerbach,* 8, in *Selected Writings* (Moscow: Progress Publishers, 1989) 15.
2. Karl Rahner, *Foundations of Christian Faith* (New York: Crossroad, 1984) 46.
3. Ibid, 44.
4. Ibid, 49.
5. Georges Bataille, *Theory of Religion,* trans. Robert Hurley (New York: Zone Books, 1992) 57.
6. Rahner, *Foundations,* 51.
7. I agree that this 'common agreement' may be rejected by some in the name of pluralism. However, I do not consider pluralism an unconditional value, and where it degenerates into a cacophony of Babel-like incommunication some form of agreement may be required in its place.
8. Harvey Cox, *Religion in the Secular City: Towards a Postmodern Theology* (New York: Simon and Schuster, 1984) 168.
9. See Juan Luis Segundo, 'Two Theologies of Liberation', *The Month* 17:10 (1984) 321-27, where he outlines tensions in the work of some liberation theologians between their reluctance to reject popular piety and their critique of many of its misapprehensions of Christian belief.
10. I have attempted elsewhere to show how at least one form of contemporary thinking can both offer a critique of the function of a religious tradition while also helping to retrieve the tradition and forge a critical theology. See my 'Foucault on Continuity: the postmodern challenge to tradition', *Faith and Philosophy,* 9:3 (July, 1992) 335-352.
11. See George Lindbeck, *The Nature of Doctrine: Religion and Theology in a Postliberal Age* (Philadelphia: Westminster Press, 1984) 63-72. I do not agree with everything in Lindbeck's 'post-liberal theology', but I do concur with this description of the truth of religious language.
12. Lindbeck, *The Nature of Doctrine,* 65.
13. Ibid. Of course religious language differs from other, non-re-

ligious, forms of performative speech; but religious language is unique in requiring both a pre-existing reality (God) and a context of human words and actions to make that (non-empirical) reality 'present'.

CHAPTER THIRTEEN

The Politics of Idolatry

Paul Surlis

Atheism and secularisation are often presented as the great threats to faith and religion at the present time. Less often are we told that *idolatry*, that is false worship of the true God or worship of false gods, is a major threat not only to faith and religious belief but to the well-being of millions of concrete human beings in our world. Should atheism be condemned totally and outright even where it is combined with wide-ranging concern for the poor and marginalised? Should not rather the focus of concern be on that false religious practice – really idolatry – that pays lip service to God and religious values while suppressing calls for social justice and the systemic changes necessary to provide for the survival needs of the impoverished and powerless throughout the world?

We have witnessed recently the collapse of regimes where atheism was the official religion and worship of God, even in private, was proscribed. We recognise the courage and faith of people who, in such hostile circumstances, nourished belief in God and sustained it in themselves and in their children without benefit of organised religion. However, we need to recall that sometimes the godlessness or atheism of, for example communist systems, has been used to conceal or discredit the genuine thrust towards social justice contained in these regimes and most clearly evident in Cuba and Nicaragua. In these countries (and also to a lesser extent in the former Soviet Union and in China) food, clothing, shelter, education, employment and healthcare were provided to the majority on the basis of need, not on the basis of ability to pay. Matthew's gospel (25:31-46) favourably judges the nations that made these human survival needs their primary concern. Nations that *professed* belief in God and Jesus, but neglected their social obligations to the needy, are condemned for religious practice that was vacuous and false.

Capitalism and the free-market are being hailed as the saviours of the modern world after fifty years of suspicion, hostility and vast militarisation. But it is now becoming clear, with the publication of documents relating to the real intent of Cold War propaganda, that the perceived and feared threat was that presented by socialist regimes to capitalism as an economic system and to the social formations it needs and engenders. But since these social formations are often oppressive, violent and unjust, the threat was disguised and presented in terms of denial of freedom and cherished 'Christian values.'

The decade which included the Reagan presidency (1980-1990) saw the US military industrial complex expend two trillion dollars enlarging and expanding the US military arsenal. To justify this vast expenditure, president Reagan referred to the USSR as the evil empire. This political Manichaeism enabled Reagan to expand the military budget excessively and to cut social programmes, especially those dealing with children, women, persons of colour and their very survival needs.

Moreover, president Reagan, utilising the CIA and covert agencies, pursued what is called Low Intensity Conflict (LIC) in several Latin American Countries. LIC involves using local military forces trained, financed and armed by the US Pentagon to fight guerrillas in their own countries. Terrorism, torture, 'disappearancing' of civilians, bombing and mining, were used to terrify and subdue people fighting for land, housing, employment, education and healthcare. LIC had the 'advantage' for the Reagan administration that it could be deployed without encountering much anti-war sentiment in the US itself. LIC was successfully used to topple the Sandinistas in Nicaragua at the cost of 30,000 lives and $17 billion to the Sandinista economy. In El Salvador eighty thousand persons were murdered, and in Guatemala 70,000 mostly native peoples (Indians) were destroyed because they dared to struggle for social justice. But US propaganda declared that these wars were pursued in defence of western civilisation and its Christian values. And so an East-West religious interpretation (East = Soviet, atheistic communism, West = Christian, US) was given to what in reality was a North-South economic issue with political and cultural dimensions. Seeing the matter in North-South terms essentially involves recognising that what was really at stake in El Salvador, Nicaragua, Guatemala, was continued access to cheap labour, cheap resources and slack environmental laws – hence greater profit for capitalist transnational corporations and the minority who benefit from them. What the US did in Central and South America in destroying social justice-oriented uprisings had the support of most Western democracies, or at least was seldom effectively resisted by them. Since what was done was perpetrated in the name of God and Christian civilisation, the issue is theological and not purely political.

Fear of and hatred for godless communism was also used very effectively in South Africa, and in other parts of Africa as well as in Asia, during the past fifty years or so. Persecution of religion by regimes in Eastern Europe, the Soviet Union and China lent credence to the anticommunist 'Christian' propaganda but often ignored was the social conversatism of the churches and their failure to work effectively for systemic social change in the interests of the powerless and downtrodden.

William A. Wilson, the first US Ambassador to the Holy See, has recently spoken about the mutual collaboration of the United States and the Vatican in defence of their respective interests in parts of Africa and Central and South America. The US and the Vatican both saw liberation theology as more of a political than a religious problem, though it had elements of both. In recent interviews quoted in the *New York Times* and elsewhere, Wilson informs us that the Vatican attacked and silenced liberation theologians for political as well as theological reasons. In return, the US dropped programmes funding birth control and abortion from its foreign policy agenda. Thus prophetic religious persons, lay people, sisters, priests and bishops were sacrificed in the interests of imperial power by the court theologians who hold power at the global level today.

What we are dealing with here evokes a classic biblical theme: the battle of the gods, or Yahweh's struggle against false gods.

Most Latin American liberation theologians interpret their politico-religious situation not exclusively in terms of atheism or secularism or existential loss of meaning. Rather they see idolatry as a central issue. They see false worship of the true God, pseudo-concern for Christian values, legitimating a crushing system of injustice and exploitation. These false gods and idols are powerfully effective because they masquerade under the guise of respect for the true God, for religion and religious values, and yet everything they stand for is destructive of millions of concrete human persons and their life-sustaining environment.

Theology, especially 'naming God', is a location of conflict within Christian churches in many areas of the world today. In these churches, many women see a core symbol system that is male-oriented and male dominated. Women see dogmas, structures and institutions that use monarchical God concepts to consolidate patriarchy and an exclusively male priesthood or ministry. These in turn help, in the Catholic Church, to disempower women and most men whom Vatican officials appear intent on keeping in a quasi-infantile state as far as many aspects of religion – especially its sexual morality – are concerned. The denial of even the right to discuss the validity of ordaining women to priesthood causes pain and distress. And insofar as the male anatomy of Christ is the final obstacle to women being priests, this is seen as implausible nonsense if not outright heresy.

Some critics of Vatican politics of religion see that a form of *papolatry*, or quasi-idolatrous veneration of the Pope, has been engendered and this in turn is used to legitimate religious authority which is exercised in dictatorial fashion. A fetish is made out of obedience, and legitimate dissent (in sexual ethics and certain areas of belief) is condemned as if it were demonic.

Idolatrous destruction of life in pursuit of economic or political advantage is inextricably entwined with religious oppression, with its fetishes and idols. When we, who are representatives of religion, fail to discern and denounce false gods in the public arena, we support political repression with its violence, torture, murder, enforced impoverishment and ecological destruction which destroys the well-being of millions of people today.

The Bible condemns all forms of idolatry in the name of Yahweh, the true God who is best described as liberator. Pablo Richard correctly argues that only the slave and the oppressor are idolatrous. (*The Idols of Death and the God of Light: A Theology*, Pablo Richard et al, New York: Orbis, 1980.) Commenting on the

Golden Calf episode of Exodus 32, Richard argues that the sinfulness of the idolatry does not lie in the attempt to make God material or visible. Richard concedes that the transcendence of God is at stake, but he understands transcendence not as referring to God's spiritual being but as referring to God as liberator. 'The sin against the transcendence of God ... consisted in the people's refusal of its own liberation and in the construction of a false liberation through the alienating worship of a god who would console them but not set them free' (p. 7). Wishing to emphasise orthopraxis, Richard continues: 'God the liberator is always a god who transcends human impossibilities, always the god of hope against all hope, always the god who will not tolerate the fear and alienation that the oppressor has installed in the oppressed people' (p. 7).

Richard, and other theologians of liberation, take God's plan for historical human liberation with utmost seriousness. Refusal to struggle for socio-political liberation, or to view it as utterly beyond human reach, is tantamount to idolatrous behaviour. Equating belief in divine transcendence primarily with refusal to be limited or bound by oppressive socio-economic, political or cultural conditions of oppression, implies rejection as idolatrous of the god who only consoles the oppressed so that they accept fatalistically their sub-human status. Richard asserts correctly, apropos of Exodus 32, that the throne of the consoling god is '...gold and gold is the symbol of domination' (p. 7).

John W. deGruchy, a South-African liberation theologian, writes '...if idolatry is something on which we bestow divine honours, or in Juan Luis Segundo's words the 'absolutization of what is false', then it applies to whatever we give our ultimate allegiance and which in turn shapes our values and lifestyle ... Moreover, idols are never neutral; they are inevitably co-opted to legitimate the immoralities of their worshippers, and especially those that pertain to their material interests.' (*Liberating Reformed Theology: A South African Contribution to an Ecumenical Debate*, Michigan: Eerdmans, 1991, p. 103)

Prophetic religion links knowing and serving the true God with the struggle for justice in social and personal relationships. M. Douglas Meeks, in *God the Economist: The Doctrine of God and Political Economy* (Minneapolis: Fortress Press, 1989), writes about

God's concern for the material as well as the spiritual well-being of all persons. God as householder (the original meaning of *economist*) like any good parent, is concerned that all God's off-spring have food, clothing, shelter, education, healthcare, and employment, because without these things persons are diminished and disfigured or die of neglect. The glory of God is the human person fully alive, and the material conditions necessary to sustain life with dignity and with regard to environmental resources are of concern to God, as the Bible makes abundantly clear.

And yet we know how appallingly otherwise the case is today for masses of people in all countries but especially in large parts of Asia, Africa and Latin America. The poorest of the poor are always women and children, especially women and children of colour. There are many oppressions in our world among which sexism, racism, classism, militarism, are some of the worst and most destructive. It is perhaps insidious to select whether, among systemic oppressions today, capitalism or patriarchy is most fundamental. It can be argued that a major determining cause of destructive violence, poverty, war and death today is capitalism utilising patriarchy, racism and militarism to provide an inherently exploitative global socio-economic system that is driven by a quest for ever-increasing profit and the prestige and power it brings. The New Testament names Mammon as a paradigm of all idolatry and is unambiguous in stating: 'You cannot serve God and mammon' (Mt 6:24) where mammon refers to relentless pursuit of, and absolute trust in, wealth. Calvin said, 'All covetous men must deny God and put wealth in his place' (cited in deGruchy, p. 104). Exploitation under capitalism does not come only from greed or covetousness but from the logic of the system which entails the production of ever-increasing profit. It is clear today that logic requires the commodification of land, labour and the resources needed for human survival. It would appear that we need the market mechanism but we must situate it within political, social and cultural frameworks of restraint so that the production process and the market become instruments of human and ecological well-being, not instruments of human and environmental destruction.

Speaking analogously, it is not far-fetched to suggest that modern transnational corporations, and the systems that protect their interests, operate today with power that is absolute. Their interests – ever-increasing profits and the power and status that profit brings – are absolutised and they devour human life and cause starvation, poverty, unemployment and ecological destruction within nations and globally. Biblically inspired prophets would, I believe, discern false gods here and would denounce them accordingly. They would not, nor should we, suggest that the capitalist system can retain its logic but can be humanised around the edges.

We often decry the privatisation of religion in modern times. We fail, however, to examine a central structural cause mandating such privatisation. The logic of capitalism precludes public, national, or global success in feeding the hungry, clothing the naked, of providing for the survival needs of all children, women and men. Basic justice on a global scale is impossible under capitalism as the history of the past four hundred years shows. This, I believe, is why persons of good will are forced to practice private virtue and privatised religion, and why making and keeping human life more human is becoming more impossible even as knowledge, technology and science improve. If we say the system cannot be changed or replaced, we are succumbing to fatalism and idolatry. We are summoned by God to struggle for the liberation of all persons from sin and from all that oppresses them. The politics of idolatry is enslaving and death-dealing. The politics of God is liberative and life-enhancing, and to this fidelity to gospel values calls us today.

PART IV

The Christian Understanding of God in the Context of the World Religions

CHAPTER FOURTEEN

The Challenge of Interfaith Dialogue to the Christian Understanding of God

Ursula King

The title of our colloquium, 'The Christian Understanding of God Today' is closely connected with our Western way of thinking which is deeply wedded to an intellectual project where conceptual clarification and rational understanding are at the centre of our approach to the world and ourselves. Thus the 'understanding' of the title is too often understood in a rather abstract and limited conceptual way which can also imprison the way we perceive what may be a challenge to our traditional ways of understanding. My immediate reply to a question about the challenge of interfaith dialogue to the Christian *understanding* of God would be to say that it is not so much the challenge of *understanding*, though that is there too, but that the greatest challenge comes from the different ways of *experiencing* the divine mystery at the heart of the universe – experiences which are linked to different visions, perceptions and worldviews which find expression in a multitude of concepts, religious and theological traditions.

Michael Barnes has published a short study on *God East and West* (London: SPCK, 1991) wherein he rightly draws attention to the personal dimensions of one's own journey of understanding and the difficulty of speaking about the Ultimate in human terms, as we must, even when we have the ancient resources of an ancient religious tradition at our disposal. His own reflections on the Christian, Hindu and Buddhist approaches to the Divine Mystery draw attention to the limits of language in 'what in the West we call with easy casualness 'God' and in the East by a whole variety of terms' (page 5).

I have not been asked to address my remarks to any particular dialogue which has developed between Christians and members of other specific faith communities, but to reflect on the challenge of interfaith dialogue in general. Other contributors will speak on aspects of Christian-Buddhist, Christian-Muslim dialogue as well as Christian encounters in Asia where most of my experience also stems from.

The challenge of dialogue for Christian theology and the Christian churches has become public and more prominent during the last twenty to thirty years, with considerable visibility and credibility given to dialogue by the declarations of the Second Vatican Council and the World Council of Churches. But at a personal level, and in a more limited way, the challenge of dialogue has existed in Christian missionary circles for several hundred years, since the time when Western Christian missionaries first encountered the different religious beliefs and practices which sustained the lives of people in China, India and Japan. It was this challenge of different cultures and societies which freed the European mind from its insularity and narrowness. But from the beginning it also included the challenge of how to know and speak about the Ultimate in human terms in ways profoundly different from the Christian understanding of a trinitarian and incarnate God. We are heirs to these historical encounters and discussions, whether they took place in a confrontational or conciliatory setting. Much of this historical context has still to be worked through and clarified. That is true of contemporary dialogue, too, for though it has much advanced, it is still in its initial phases regarding a full understanding of the significance of religious pluralism and interfaith dialogue. What affect will this have on the global transformation of religious communities, their self-understanding, religious practices and theological reflections in twenty or thirty years? These questions remain unanswerable at present, but as far as the challenge of dialogue to the Christian understanding of God is concerned, I tentatively propose three ways in which this challenge expresses itself and invites a response from us: A new experiencing of the Divine *around* us; a new naming of God *among* us; a new encounter of the presence of the Spirit *within* us and *within* our communities.

1. A new experiencing of the Divine around us

Ever since Rudolph Otto formulated his idea of 'the Numinous' following his experience of fascination, wonder and awe in a Jewish synagogue and a North African mosque, scholars have looked for comparative elements of the Divine and the Holy, experienced and expressed in religious traditions other than our own. Partaking in the worship of another community can be a powerfully transformative experience, and it is not without reason that some are afraid of it and wish to rule it out of court as too threatening at the core. It is an experience which is open to many of us today, whether through the presence of different religious communities among us, or through travel, or in an indirect way through the media of film and television. Even at that distant, mediated level the challenge must not be taken lightly for it can open one's awareness to the otherness of a different religious orientation and focus.

If more knowledge and a different engagement in interfaith dialogue are sought, then a whole host of questions is likely to arise: about God, prayer, meditation, sacred texts, religious communities, and codes of conduct for one's life. By passing over into another faith and then returning to one's own, one becomes transformed and understands one's faith anew. In my experience, the most difficult differences, and the hardest to resolve do not occur at the level of theological encounter regarding God, faith or prayer, but at the level of human conduct and the organisation of family and society. Here the differences are much sharper, more exclusive and more painful. And yet practical differences are undergirded by and grounded in important and difficult theological distinctions and different approaches to *truth*.

The encounter with other experiences and expressions of the Divine whether through worship, textual study of scriptures and commentaries, or through theological reflection, opens up tremendous possibilities if it is approached as potentially fruitful and enriching rather than feared as threatening and destructive. Thus the very perception of what the challenge consists in, and how it can best be met, depends to a great extent on one's existential, moral and intellectual choices and one's willingness to take on ventures and risk.

A great challenge arises from the new discovery of God's immanence in the world, in creation, in the cosmos – a challenge opened up through the great reverence for nature and all forms of life present in eastern religions, but also a challenge which arises through the new insights of the life sciences, astronomy, cosmology and the development of ecological concern. With the renewed emphasis on the cosmic roots and dimensions of human existence, new questions about the relationship between cosmos and history have been asked and new perspectives have been explored about the world as the body of God. Here we find rich food for thought in Hindu and Buddhist speculations, and it is not surprising that some Christian theologians in India have shown a special interest in developing a theology of the cosmic Christ, whereas Western writers have begun to write about the world as God's body, a theme central to the medieval Hindu theologian Ramanuja.

With a new experience of and a new sensibility for the richness of both our natural and social environment, we seek new theological expressions to make sense of and give meaning to our new experiences in the light of our Christian history and tradition. This leads me to my next point.

2. *A new naming of God among us*

Many contemporary theologians call for a metamorphosis in our naming of God, whether they are coming from a background in feminist, political or liberation theology. Here and elsewhere in theological thinking we come upon a profound paradigm shift in the way theology is understood and practised. Through the development of a critical hermeneutics, theologians re-examine the very foundations of Western theology itself. The old name of 'God', pronounced with such casualness and a frequent assumption that its meaning can be taken for granted, has become an imprisoned symbol for many, a name whose limited function is being recognised and whose usefulness is being questioned. Feminist theologians are not alone in calling for a new naming of God, for new models and metaphors more pregnant with meaning. Of course we possess many names and images for God in the Bible. We have a rich heritage of Christian apophatic and kataphatic mysticism, but one must recognise that in spite of this there is probably no other language as rich as Sanskrit which presents many more distinct terms and concepts with which to capture the myriad aspects of Ultimate Reality, of the Divine Mystery, emphatically proclaimed to be one in spite of all contrary appearances. It is this experimental, conceptual and linguistic richness of the Indian religious tradition which is one of the greatest challenges to the Christian understanding of God. This challenge has engaged several western Christians at the deepest level of reflection, whether one thinks of Pere Monchanin, Raymond Panikkar, Bede Griffith, or Swami Abhishiktananda who explored the comparison between the Christian understanding of the Trinity and Indian perception of Brahman as *saccidananda.*

Hindu theology includes highly developed reflections on the impersonal and personal forms of the Divine. India also possesses a prolific 'visual theology' expressed in images and statues throughout the subcontinent and now also among Hindu communities abroad. These visual expressions are linked to a theology of 'seeing', of *darshan,* a sight and vision graciously granted to the worshipper. At the heart of Hindu worship there lies an exchange of mutuality and vision – a seeing which is not only a passive awareness but requires an active focussing so that *darshan* connotes a special mode of knowing, an insight which at times can unfold into a vision – a seeing, touching, tasting and naming of divine glory, experienced by humans in all its contradictions – as found in the famous theophany of chapter eleven of the Bhagavad Gita.[1] It comes as no surprise that Rudolph Otto singled out this chapter as one of the great visions in world religious literature, nor that Western readers of the Gita, ever since it was first translated into English in 1785, have compared the vision of God in the Gita, who is both Krishna and the universal cosmic Vishnu, with the Christian understanding of God in the New Testament.

3. The Spirit within us and within our communities

We encounter a profound challenge to our traditional Christian understanding of God by meeting the theology and worship of other faiths. This challenge can perhaps be best summed up as the challenge of the Spirit among us. 'Signs of the Spirit' was the motto of the VII WCC Assembly in Canberra. One of the two plenary speakers on the theme 'Come Holy Spirit – Renew the Whole Creation' was the Korean woman professor Chung Hyun Kyung who created a stir and much discussion, not only because of the stark concreteness and feminist approach in dealing with her topic, but also because she emphasised, as Asian Christian women theologians tend to do, a particular sensitivity to the religious pluralism and spiritual heritage of Asia. When calling on the Holy Spirit to break down our walls of division with wisdom and compassion, she pointed to the Buddhist image of *Kannon,* the Bodhisattva of compassion and wisdom which in East Asia is depicted in female form.[2]

We need the energy, the creativity, the transforming, enabling, nurturing power of the Spirit of God to transform ourselves and our communities. This is a cry widely voiced. This is the challenge of *ruach*, of *sophia*, of *pneuma*, the divine Spirit of Wisdom – a vision of God not fully explored yet in either our own tradition or in the living experience and witness of other faiths. Our God has traditionally been too much a God of righteousness and justice, a God of distant majesty and severe judgement. Yet through the incarnation we also have a God of nearness and lowliness, a God of suffering and pain, a God of intimate love and vulnerability, some aspects of which are paralleled in the Hindu God Krishna and the doctrine of the *avatars*.

The Indian understanding of God also includes a deep appreciation of the elements of joy and bliss, of divine superabundance and creativity which are the work of the Spirit, together with the strength of compassionate wisdom.

These are ancient insights but the meeting of people from different religious traditions in East and West is a new experience, the sign of a new season in human history. Many speak of a newly emerging spirituality, not least in Asia, among Christians who are reflecting afresh on the Christian message within the new context of interfaith encounter and religious pluralism. As Professor Chung Hyun Kyung has rightly remarked, theologians have often fallen prey to the violence of abstraction; we need all the powers of our spiritual and theological imagination to be attentive to the voice of God's Spirit, learn anew to praise God's presence among us, and seek a new understanding of God within the multiple contexts of our complex world.

Notes

1. I have explored this more fully in 'Darshan - Seeing the Divine: The Meeting of Hindu and Christian Experience.' The Fifth Lambeth Interfaith Lecture, published by *The Centre for the Study of Religion and Society Pamphlet Library* (University of Kent, 1986, Lecture 11).

2. See the full text in Michael Kinnamon, ed., *Signs of the Spirit,* Official Report Seventh Assembly, Canberra, 7-20 February 1991 (Geneva: WCC Publications, 1991) A fuller introduction to Chung Hyun Kyung's work is found in her book *Struggle be the Sun Again: Introducing Asian Women's Theology* (London: SCM Press, 1991).

CHAPTER FIFTEEN

Some Aspects of Buddhist-Christian Dialogue

David Tracy

For the last seven years I have been involved in Buddhist-Christian dialogue with ten Christian theologians and ten Buddhist thinkers, who meet once a year. Since our colloquium is on God I will make some suggestions as to what difference this dialogue has made for me. I have a certain hesitation, as the two organisers of the Buddhist-Christian dialogue in which I am involved, the Christian theologian John Cobb and the Buddhist thinker Masao Abe, did not allow us to speak about God and emptiness for the first two years. The first year the dialogue was on 'What is the problem?'; so the Christians had to talk about what they thought was awry and what they meant by sin, and the Buddhists on *Avijja,* or primal ignorance. The second year was on 'What is enlightenment?' and 'What is redemption?'; and only then were we allowed to talk about God.

Buddhist-Christian dialogue has proved to be one of the most puzzling and fruitful attempts at genuine dialogue in our curious period. It is exceptionally fruitful, in my opinion, insofar as it allows the Christian to acknowledge the other as genuinely Other, and not as a projection of Christian self-identity, as often occurs, because of the troubled history, in the Christian understanding of the Jew; and in both the Christian and Jewish (and even Islamic) understanding of those they call 'the pagan'. Here in the Buddhist dialogue the other has a chance to be genuinely Other, and not a projection of oneself. For the Christian or Jew, finally, what can be more other than this Buddhist Other who names ultimate reality not with the word 'God' but with *Sunyata* or 'emptiness'. This Other that declares that there is no self, or more exactly with Nagarjuna (far more radical than Derrida, in fact) that both self and no-self neither exist nor do not exist. This Buddhist Other who, in any conversation one has, will immediately employ a highly metaphysical vocabulary on being and non-being, and who at the same time will insist on the need for a radical suspicion of all metaphysical and theological language; and indeed, at the limit, all language. This Buddhist Other who insists that the more familiar Western analogical and dialectical languages of philosophy and theology alike may be unable to rid Western thought of those dualisms that allegedly distort all our thought. This Buddhist Other who, in many ways, has become the preferred Other of many postmodern thinkers in our period – just as for the eighteenth-century Enlightenment thinkers a Western version of neo-Confucianism (or China) and for the Romantics a Western version of India and the archaic traditions became preferred Others. This is, of course, a difficulty and not a solution.

At the same time Buddhist thinkers often employ brilliant dialectical strategies (classically in Nagarjuna) or develop analogical relationships such as in modern Kyoto Buddhist thinkers (e.g. Nishitani) in order to insist upon a non-dialectical and non-analogical non-dualist form of thought. For healing, even salvific insight here consists in acknowledging all reality as neither one nor many, but as *not-two.* The Jew and the Christian, faithful to their prophetic heritage, attempt to continue to live the peculiar Christian dialectic of a responsible self before a covenanting, responding God. Thus do they learn that they are attempting to be freed *from* the world *for* the world, as in the great prophetic traditions and trajectories of Judaism and Christianity.

The Buddhist, in an analogous but ultimately quite different way, insists that enlightenment to true *Nirvana* (enlightenment) also includes the acknowledgement that *Nirvana* and *Samsara* (the world of illusion) are one. For the Buddhist must not cling to the ego, must not even cling to non-clinging; she or he should not cling to enlightenment or to an understanding of reality as emptiness if he or she is to be enlightened. In an extraordinary move, unfamiliar in my judgment to any form of Western thought – to the Platonist or the Stoic, much less classic Jewish or Christian thought, or their later forms of analogical or dialectical thought – the Buddhist analysis of the human dilemma suggests that the very problem that is signalled for attention – namely not guilt but transience – becomes for the no-self (i.e. the non-clinging, enlightened one) the solution. This extraordinary suggestion that transience is both the problem and the solution – a way at once peculiarly Buddhist and, oddly, postmodern for many Western thinkers – has been glimpsed by very few in the Western Christian tradition. Perhaps this way is what Ernst Troeltsch in his unjustly neglected *Glaubenslehre* (which, alas, came out just as Barth took over) was struggling to articulate. Troeltsch was one of the few Christian theologians for whom the transience of Western culture and Western Christianity was so central. He had a profound sense of the importance of transience as an issue for thoughtful Westerners, indeed perhaps as a principal question for any thoughtful late-modern Western theological inquirer. Perhaps as Christianity itself ceases to be a Eurocentric religion and becomes finally a truly world church, this Buddhist insight into the religious meaning of transience may help Christians to let go of their compulsive clingings to what are finally transient ways of understanding God and action.

The Eckhart-Ruuysbroec Debate and Sunyata

The Buddhist-Christian dialogue may also help many, as it helped me on the question of God, to return to the radically apophatic, mystical traditions in Christianity, especially that most curious of Christian thinkers, and the preferred Christian thinker by Buddhists, inevitably, Meister Eckhart. Eckhart remains the clearest *analogue* in the Christian tradition to the kind of radically kenotic interpretation of the Christian understanding of God articulated by some Buddhist thinkers.

The true God for the Christian, the God of the prophets and of Jesus the Christ, is the One to whom one owes loyalty and trust. But the true God can become merely some projected Other to whom we egotistically cling – and Christians, when honest, will admit to our clinging, to our refusal to let go of the law of infinite desire, to our inability to understand God because of our refusal to face the radical transience even of our best categories which can finally terrorise us. When even prophetic denunciations of our idolatries cannot break through such compulsive clinging to an ultimately idolatrous God in prophetic terms, then the modern Christian theologian listening to the challenge of the Buddhist insight that belief in God can at times be a more subtle form of egotistic clinging, may rejoin even Meister Eckhart in his famous prayer 'I pray to God to free me from God'. The 'Godhead beyond God' of Eckhart is a possible, and perhaps for some thoughtful Christians in the postmodern situation, a salutary theological move for anyone concerned to learn to try to live both like and, inevitably, unlike a Buddhist in a situation of radical transience, where Eckhart's famous motto – 'to live without a Why' – becomes a genuine option for the Christian. Perhaps this is the sense which Thomas Merton was urging upon his readers at the end of his life when he suggested that Christians need to learn Zen forms of meditation and attempt to become what is needed in the new century, namely what he called 'self-transcending Christians'.

What strikes a reader most today, I think, about texts like Eckhart's – which I admit I could never read before I participated in Buddhist-Christian dialogue; I found them simply odd – is the spirituality (or, religious awareness) that is marked above all by two characteristics: intellectualism and a radical sense of detachment. And here a rigorous intellectualism not only is not divorced from spirituality but is a central expression of it. For Eckhart, many suggest, this shows his fidelity to his Dominican tradition, in contrast to the greater love-orientation of the Franciscans and many others. And when that kind of detachment takes over, what happens to your understanding of God? This Eckhartian spirituality bears remarkable resemblance to the non-attachment, non-clinging spirituality of all forms of Buddhism despite their other very important differences. Like the Buddhist and unlike love-oriented Christians, including the mystics, Eckhart sometimes seems to accord something like, and I hesitate here, a 'different' and perhaps even 'higher' spiritual role to the sense of detachment. This causes serious consequences for an attempt to think about God, including the Trinity. On the one hand, he is far more apophatic in his language than even such apophatically inclined love-mystics as John of the Cross. On the other hand, unlike some but by no means all Christian mystics, Eckhart is clearly not interested in intense experiences like rapture or ecstasy, but rather like Buddhists is far more interested in detached experiences allowing true awareness of the everyday. In the Buddhist case *Nirvana* and *Samsara* are one. In Eckhart's case, the disclosure of the Godhead beyond God is, at the same time, the disclosure of our release to the everyday life of activity-in-the-world. His remarkable reading of the Martha-Mary story is especially illustrative here for, in his reading, it is the active-contemplative Martha and not (as for many Christian contemplatives) the purely contemplative Mary who is the best illustration of the Christian contemplative's life.

These affinities (not *identities*) in the kind of spiritual awareness of Eckhart and Zen make plausible the appeal of Eckhart to Buddhist thinkers. That same kind of spirituality of radical detachment and intellectualism leads to some of the more radically apophatic conceptualities of Eckhart, especially his famous insistence on the 'Godhead beyond God' wherein even the names Father, Son and Spirit are deemed inappropriate. Although Eckhart does not make this characteristic move in the kenotic lines favoured by some Buddhist thinkers, he does make it in such a manner that the language of nothingness receives an unusual radicality for a Christian thinker. To be sure, as Buddhist thinkers have been quick to note, even Eckhart's 'nothingness' is not the 'absolute nothingness' of Zen thought.

That this is true can be seen in the fact that, however radically apophatic Eckhart is for a Christian thinker, he remains a God-obsessed thinker who constantly shifts, in different contexts, his language of transcendentals for both God and the Godhead beyond God: not only Nothingness but One, Intelligence, and *Esse* seem to him appropriate if always inadequate language. Whether all Eckhart's language can be rendered coherent without either loss of all *Christian* God-language or without reducing his position to some more familiar Christian understanding of God remains the principal question still under dispute.

One of the things, in my judgment, that happens in any serious dialogue – besides discovering, if you are honest in the dialogue, Otherness – is also rediscovering or discovering for the first time, as in my case with Eckhart, aspects of your own tradition which made no sense to you before. And one of the classic debates in Christian theology, which is not often discussed, even in trinitarian debates, is the discussion between Eckhart and the slightly later figure of Jan Ruuysbroec, and it's a discussion whether this language of 'the Godhead beyond God' is finally a language that is beyond the Trinity, as sometimes Eckhart suggests, or, as Ruuysbroec suggests, is finally itself that kind of apophaticism disclosive of a trinitarian understanding of reality as love and as wisdom.

Although I remain puzzled whether the Christian understanding of God can receive as radically an apophatic character as Eckhart sometimes insists upon, it is possible that Eckhart's 'Godhead beyond God' language may be appropriate Christian theological language – not merely in the relatively easy sense of one way to acknowledge the radical inadequacy of all our God-language, but in the more difficult dialectical sense of a more adequate naming of what Christians call God. For that reason, at this time and prior to further reflection impelled by the Buddhist-Christian dialogue and the rethinking of the apophatic tradition, I find myself, in Christian theological terms, more with Jan Ruuysbroec than with Meister Eckhart. One may furnish the Christian theological reasons to move in Ruuysbroec's direction for understanding the Christian God in terms of both spirituality and theology. In the Christian spiritual life, the move to radical negation and nothingness is construed by the Christian as one important moment of awareness in the larger sphere of awareness of the fuller Christian life. In the Christian construal, the most radical negation of the cloud of unknowing and the acknowledgment of nothingness must, through its own power of awareness, yield to the self-manifestation of the Divine Reality.

Theologically, this means, as Ruuysbroec clearly sees, that the radical indistinction, the no-thingness of Eckhart's Godhead-beyond-God, will necessarily manifest itself in the Christian life as the self-manifesting Father-Son-Spirit. Where Eckhart is unclear in his language about applying his diverse transcendental terms (One, *Esse*, Intelligence), sometimes to the Godhead and sometimes to the Father-Source, Ruuysbroec is clear. In Christian terms, all our language for God is inadequate. The radical negations of the spiritual life demand radical negations of all our names for God. And yet the Christian experience and thereby awareness of God's wisdom in the Logos and God's love in the Spirit remain our central clues to the reality we hesitantly name God. Insofar as Christians experience Godself as Source, Logos, and Spirit they find their central insight into God's own reality as always self-manifesting. That self-manifestation of the Father as Logos-Image is the Son. That relationship of divine manifestation is the Spirit. Christians find these conceptualities for understanding the divine reality through their very experiences and awareness of wisdom and love. Those clues to the source, order, and end of all reality allow them to name God as an always self-manifesting God – as Father-Son-Spirit (or Mother-Daughter-Spirit or Source-Logos-Spirit).

So it seems to me from the Buddhist discussion I've been in, that this classic Christian theological discussion is closely analogous to the classic Buddhist discussion, because Buddhism is not naturalism, it is not John Dewey or Santayana. It includes this awareness of ultimate reality as emptiness, as dependent origination (*Paticcasamuppada*), and at the same time as wise and compassionate. This is what intellectually needs articulation, and this is exactly the debate that you find, in my judgment, between Eckhart and Ruuysbroec, of whether trinitarian self-understanding of God is also the Christian way of understanding reality as wise and compassionate as Logos and Spirit.

Conclusion

Now clearly, even if suggestions like the ones that have emerged for many Christians and Buddhists came about – trying to understand themselves anew and trying to understand the reality of God, including the Trinitarian God in some such terms – it still of course would not in any way suggest that the Buddhist and the Christian were saying the same thing. For the Buddhist and the Christian never say finally the same thing. But the radically relational and the self-manifesting structure of ultimate reality might be commonly affirmed, and this is what is intriguing. But what if reality is radically relational and that radical relationality takes the form of Co-dependent Origination? It seems to me that that is where the real issue lies. I repeat that is why it is more like some forms of postmodern thought like Derrida, like Deleuze, like some aspects of Julia Kristeva, and others - which is both relational and non-relational. And that would render further conversation on such distinct issues as the 'duality' of God and all creatures (in the familiar Buddhist critiques of Christianity and Judaism), and the coherence of radical relationality and radically autonomous 'suchness' and its puzzling 'freedom' and 'non-freedom' (in familiar Christian critiques of Buddhism) more intelligible – or at least more discussible in mutually intelligible terms.

To find such terms of correlation is the first step needed in this great new dialogue of our day and it is extraordinary that it is trinitarian thought that also provides one way of discussing these issues of the nature of reality itself as wise and as compassionate. Christians, I think, along with Jews, cannot finally stay with the Buddhist vision. Indeed, I do not believe that one can even finally stay with Meister Eckhart. But only those who have allowed the challenge of the otherness of Eckhart from within the tradition and the Buddhist from without to be real, like a Ruuysbroec or a Nicholas of Cusa did, are likely to lead us further in the kind of theological attempts to rename God now needed, as in Eckhart's profound reflections on the namings of the One. Similarly, I believe, only those Christians in an emerging world-church in a polycentric global culture who are willing to listen to the challenge of the otherness of the Buddhist way, a way that has also now become a Western way and is no longer simply an Eastern way, can move us further along the route that we all probably still need to take – what might be called the *mystical-prophetic journey* – where the inter-religious dialogue will become an integral part of all serious Christian theological thought, at least those forms of Christian theological thought like liberation, political and feminist theologies which attempt to intrinsically relate (as Gutierrez and others correctly insist) the mystical and the prophetic heritage in the renamings of God. In this regard it is interesting that Buddhists, especially the Japanese Buddhists, say that what they have found most unsettling and troublesome and transformative about speaking to Christians is that Christians do try to put together love and justice – that does not mean we successfully do it – but every Christian who is serious knows that if you speak only about love you are probably going to end up sentimental and if you speak only about justice you are probably going to end up self-righteous. And if you can't find a serious way in living and in thought of putting those together you are not faithful to the Christian dialectic.

Clearly the Buddhist and the Christian are not going the same way, but perhaps neither are we in any obvious way two, merely one other to one another. Perhaps as the Buddhist suggests we are neither the same nor other, but *not two*. Only a further dialogue might tell.[1]

Notes

1. I have developed some of these ideas in more detail in 'Kenosis, Sunyata, Trinity: A Dialogue with Masao Abe', in *The Emptying God: A Buddhist-Christian Conversation,* John B. Cobb, Jr. and Christopher Ives, eds (Maryknoll: Orbis, 1990) 135-154.

CHAPTER SIXTEEN

The Trinity in Melanesia:

Understanding the Christian God in a Pacific Culture

John D'Arcy May

It is one thing to discuss the Trinity in the security of a European tradition – whether of the Latin West or of Eastern Orthodoxy – for which this doctrine represents the basic coinage of all theological discourse. It is quite another to contemplate the introduction of such a revolutionary religious idea into a culture in which it was utterly alien. This is what happened many times over in the Pacific, and the result not only provides the anthropologist with fascinating case studies in cultural interaction, it also affords the theologian an opportunity to re-examine the doctrine of the Trinity from a functional point of view. The Pacific, with its generally pragmatic and life-affirming cultures, should have unlocked the liberative potential which recent theology tells us is characteristic of the 'social doctrine of the Trinity'. Did this in fact happen?

In order to avoid undue generalisation, I should like to restrict myself to the area of the south-west Pacific known to anthropologists – and to the islanders themselves as their regional awareness develops – as Melanesia. The evangelisation of the Pacific in the nineteenth century took the form of a missionary wave which swept triumphantly from east to west. In Polynesia, with its hierarchically ordered societies and supreme deities such as the Maori 'Io', acceptance of the new faith was generally enthusiastic and its effects permanent, so much so that today the rhythm of church life is inseparable from culture and society in island nations such as Tonga and Western Samoa. But the wave of evangelism foamed to a halt when it reached the 'dark islands' to the north-west which had never been seriously explored by Westerners. A climate inhospitable even to other Pacific Islanders; the harsh terrain of deep valleys and impenetrable jungles; proud and aggressive peoples for whom constant warfare was a way of life; and not least the bewildering variety of one fifth of all the languages spoken on earth, seven hundred of them in present-day

Papua New Guinea alone: even for veterans of other mission fields Melanesia presented a daunting challenge.[1] Often rebuffed by the tiny, self-contained 'survival units' which constituted Melanesian societies, the early missionaries were often unable to see anything 'religious' in the rites and customs they encountered. European anthropology was to learn that its understanding of religion would be significantly expanded in the struggle to come to terms with Melanesia. Perhaps the time is coming when Western theology will follow suit.

I

Brushing aside traditional religion as primitive and depraved, the missionaries began at what was for them the beginning: the creator God of the Bible. Only much later did they realise that these peoples already knew such a God, albeit under different names (e.g. 'Anutu' on the Huon Peninsula, 'Yakili' in the Southern Highlands). Meanwhile, the missionaries agonised over how to translate the divine NAME: disregarding the Biblical precedent *YHWH Elohim Tsebaoth* (proper name-title-cognomen, as in Raamses Pharaoh 'The Great'), they usually chose what they thought was the object of the people's religious cult and used that name indifferently in all three senses. This completely overlooked the relatively minor role played by 'high gods' in comparison with 'culture heroes' such as the brothers Manub and Kilibob along the north coast of New Guinea. The missionary translators shied away from these, with the following result:

> Because the majority agreed that *Tibut Anut* was of marginal significance only, a later generation of Christians concluded that their prayers were unheard because they were delivered to the wrong address – the missionaries had fooled them into *praying to the wrong god*. So many of them switched to either God-Manub or Jesus-Kilibob respectively – but with inconclusive results.[2]

In desperation, some missionaries simply inserted the untranslated English word 'God', which meant literally nothing to the indigenes. By failing to recognise the 'indigenous trinity' of the *deus otiosus* Anut and the two brothers Manub and Kilibob, one light-skinned and the other dark, one clever and provident, the other stupid and evil (the roles and the names were sometimes exchanged), the missionaries missed a rare opportunity to reinterpret Christian faith in terms of a truly indigenous theology.

Despite these comedies of errors, the Christian message came across, powerfully – but not always the aspects of it intended by the missionaries. Jesus appeared to Melanesians as a figure of undreamed of power, with the connotations of *paua* in Melanesia and *mana* in Polynesia: a superlative source of that abundance of 'life' which is the central value in Melanesian religion. They had no difficulty connecting this with his redemptive sacrifice, because one of their most widespread myths centres around the *dema*, described as follows by Mantovani:

> a being (human or animal) is killed violently and buried (or eaten). Out of his/her/its grave comes the item of culture which stands for 'life'. The slain being is called 'dema', the local name of this being among the Marind-Alim, a culture on the south coast of [the present-day Indonesian province of] Irian Jaya ... As the dema was killed violently the shedding of blood is central to these cultures.[3]

Once the moral implications of the Christian meaning of sacrifice became clear, however, the way was open to reinterpret 'life' as a new order of peace and mutual respect between peoples who had known nothing but enmity. Among the Lutherans of the Huon Peninsula, for instance, this realisation ushered in a new social order based on the gospel, to which they gave the name *miti*.[4]

Unknown to the missionaries, however, the initial and most far-reaching impact of their preaching came from its implicit eschatology. For peoples who had never known the concept of a 'future' which could be determined by human choice or whose divine predetermination could be determined by prayer, this was a radically new idea with an unsuspected potential for social upheaval. The Melanesian view of the world is based on the efficacy of ritual. Observing that Western consumer goods continually disgorged from ships and planes as 'cargo' found their way unerringly to the whites, it was natural and logical for people to draw the conclusion that whites had superior 'magic', i.e. the correct ritual for tapping some unimaginable source of power and 'life', symbolised by material prosperity. Thus were born the famous 'cargo cults' of Melanesia, which puzzled and perplexed administrators and church leaders for a century of what the anthropologist Peter Lawrence called 'complete mutual misunderstanding'.[5] Many of the cults were fired by the expectation of an imminent 'end', sometimes heralded by the return of the renegade brother from the Manub-Kilibob myth in the person of the whites (a striking example of the radical re-shaping of a myth in order to cope with a new situation), in other cases anticipated by the building of airstrips, the setting up of markers or the opening of mountains. The newly-introduced western fetish, money, often played a key role in the ritual, as did nocturnal fertility rites in cemeteries, where it was thought the help of the ancestors could be invoked. Some cults centered around Melanesian messiahs, who consciously appropriated Christ-like attributes, even to the extent of carrying out human sacrifice (in one case before the astonished eyes of a Catholic bishop) so that the Melanesians might have 'their' messiah. More recently, the cults – now prohibited – have passed into the cultural substratum of political and economic life, though in isolated cases they still openly rival Christian churches. On the religious front they have been largely superseded by Holy Spirit movements, some of which on closer inspection betray an underlying 'cargoist' mentality: methods for the social discernment of spirits derived from traditional sorcery, an emphasis on direct experience of the Spirit, an expectation of tangible results.[6]

II

We may seem to have taken a long detour to have arrived at the doctrine of the Trinity in Melanesia, but before discussing this, it is necessary to draw out the real history of theological development in the islands as distinct from that intended by the churches. The traditional Melanesian worldview was first challenged, not by the protology of the Genesis story or the prologue of John, but by eschatology, often symbolised by apparent incidentals such as illustrations of keys or doorways in the Pidgin New Testament. Only after indigenous eschatological and messianic expectations began to ebb were they replaced by the more socially acceptable appeal of the Holy Spirit, and this continues under the (sometimes unwitting) patronage of pentecostalist groups or in an uneasy symbiosis with mainline churches.

The first outlines of a Melanesian Christology have been long in coming, but they have been worth waiting for. In a paper he delivered while still a theology student in 1976 Joe Gaqurae from the Solomon Islands painted a striking picture of Christ the Melanesian:

> As far as the pigmentation of skin is concerned, he was a Jew. The concern is that in the Melanesian eye of faith, Christ must be a Melanesian. If it was possible for Christ to become a Jew, what can stop him from becoming a Melanesian to me? If this is impossible and blasphemous then the incarnation is a false story and has no meaning for a Melanesian ... Therefore in saying that he is a Melanesian we do not mean that he is every Melanesian. He is a different Melanesian – the ideal Melanesian. The Melanesian Christ. The Ideal.[7]

From within one of the most famous cargo cults, that of Paliau Maloat of Manus, came a thoroughly indigenous reworking of the creed in the form of a divine drama involving Wing the creator, his son Wang (Jesus) and a succession of holy spirits (Wong).[8]

Under the promptings of countless latter-day evangelists and in the shadow of daunting political and ideological challenges, Melanesian theology is only at the beginning of a development which may well transform the figure of Christ in such a way as to command the attention of the wider *oikoumene*; but it is not our task to speculate on future progress.

III

The fundamental misunderstanding between missionaries and Melanesians which led to the phenomena described above and determined the development of Christian practice and theology has been analysed by Mantovani as the clash of two radically different types of religion. Allowing for confessional differences – which, significantly, seem to have had little influence on the process – the nineteenth century missionaries were theists (in some cases it may be more appropriate to say 'deists'): they were firmly convinced of the existence of a transcendent God, known by faith but demonstrable by reason. The truth of this belief was assured prior to all experience. Both the natural order and the drama of redemption were subject to the ineffable will of God, and though the doctrine of the Trinity provided as it were the 'grammar' of this faith, it was for all intents and purposes monotheistic. We may call it 'metacosmic' in order to distinguish it from Mantovani's striking characterisation of Melanesian religion as 'biocosmic', entirely focussed on the central value of 'life' by ritual involvement in the rhythms of nature, understood as both spiritual and physical. Lest we be tempted to subject this notion to some kind of Platonic idealisation, Mantovani quotes a recent anthropological description of a Melanesian culture:

> It is a religion of physiological fitness and survival. Religious goals of heightened vitality and sexual potency are achieved without recourse to sacrifice, obeisance, mediation, worship, prayer. Spirits, deities and the supernatural in general play no role ... Physical life itself, uncontrollable and frightening, is the central mystery of the religious thought of Hua males.[9]

It is the community that offers palpable proof of the power of its secret rituals to tap the wellsprings of 'life': in the fertility of its women, pigs and gardens; by the prowess of its 'big men' in the distribution of largesse, in oratory and in war; through its good relationship with the spirits of its ancestors (*tumbuna*) and of the natural environment (*masalai*). All such relationships, internal and external, human and spiritual, are maintained by networks of exchange and indebtedness based on the retributive logic of *payback* (there is no word for 'thanks' in Melanesian languages: it is more effective to keep people in your debt!). These exchange relationships take place within the framework of kin and clan, and they determine the ethical norm derived from the central religious value: what conduces to the well-being (*gutpela sindaun*) of the community – of 'our people' as the epitome of human excellence in contrast to inferior neighbours – is 'good', even if it be the exposure of twins, the abandonment of the aged or the stealing of women from other groups; what detracts from 'our' prosperity and ability to survive is ethically 'bad'.[10] Such communities do not formulate 'beliefs', nor is their ethos appropriately termed a 'faith'. The community itself, with its rituals and customs and the myths which shape them, is a single complex 'proposition' asserting in the most immediate and concrete way an internally consistent universe of ethical and religious values, the social structure articulating the cosmic order.

IV

This is the central cultural medium in which the doctrine of the Trinity would have to be expressed if it were to mean anything to Melanesians. Unpromising material, the European theologian may be tempted to remark. But just as there is no reason in principle why there cannot be reciprocal translation between Melanesian and Western languages, so also there is no absolute barrier to interreligious communication (A term I prefer, for the reasons mentioned above, to the North Atlantic commonplace 'interfaith dialogue') between the 'biocosmic' religion of Melanesia and the 'metacosmic' traditions of Christianity, even to the point of eventual mutual transformation. The doctrine of the Trinity admittedly seems to mark the limits of this possibility.

An intelligent case has been made for the proposition that Mantovani's 'biocosmism' is nothing more than 'a stress upon one element within theism rather than a separate form of religion'.[11] According to Christopher Garland, Mantovani's version of theism is truncated and individualistic; it is precisely the doctrine of the Trinity as God's self-communicating love that opens up the prospect of all life sharing in that love by being united to the being of God in the Holy Spirit.

> If 'Mana' is indeed similar to 'Life' , then such a suggestion might suggest that 'Life' is not the object of a separate form of non-theistic 'biocosmic' religion but one aspect of a theistic personal relationship with God. If that were to be the case, then it is best understood in the overall context of that relationship and not in isolation from it.[12]

A more appropriate religious symbolism than the Trinity for 'bringing together relationships, community and life', which Mantovani correctly identifies as the centrepiece of traditional religion, could scarcely be imagined.[13] Garland's proposal in support of this claim is ingenious:

> In the first place it is possible to describe communal relationships in traditional religion according to a three-fold pattern which can be used as a symbol of the Holy Trinity. The 'memory', primordial being which is the symbol of the Father, consists of the wisdom of the ancestors, to whom offerings and prayers are made in order to bring them into relationship. The

> 'understanding', expressive being which is the symbol of the Son, is the means of salvation, the plentiful supply of food produced by an effective relationship with the ancestors. The 'will', unitive being which is the symbol of the Holy Spirit is the dynamic energy, the 'mana' which flows through the relationship, making it effective.[14]

The Trinity, in short, could facilitate the awareness of individual personality whilst maintaining intact the close-knit relationships of Melanesian community.

The proposal is intriguing, but it is roundly rejected by Mantovani. He warns that it is not the job of Westerners to create theology for Melanesians, but rather to 'dismantle all the many false assumptions we fed to our Melanesian brothers and sisters through our preaching and teaching' so that they will be free to do theology their way.[15] The inferiority of Melanesian religion implied by Garland must be demonstrated from within the Melanesian symbolic system itself, not by measuring it against a Western one.

> The distortions which I expect are not proven by the fact that a religion uses a different symbolic system from the one we Westerners use in Christianity. The distortion must be proven from within the system itself. I cannot use the English grammar to prove that my German is wrong. My German will be proven wrong only by the German grammar and no other. Melanesians, I am sure both from revelation and philosophy, are likely, like any other human being, to have misunderstood and distorted God's revelation. But Melanesians must be challenged using their grammar, not the Western one.[16]

Referring to his sixteen years as a first-contact missionary among the proud Simbu people of the central highlands of Papua New Guinea, Mantovani confesses:

> Yes, my aim was to witness to a Thou who was waiting from the beginning of time for an answer in love but I had to start from where the people were, with their concerns, talking about gardens, pigs, children, spirits, rituals, etc.[17]

The 'ultimate concern' of Melanesian peoples is all-encompassing 'Life', and even if 'Christ according to my faith is LIFE pointing to the Father in the Spirit', for Melanesians this can only occur 'via the DEMA,who wanted to be killed to give true life'.[18] We may ask whether 'redemptive analogies' maybe pushed this far this fast, but even from his phenomenological point of view Mantovani is prepared to concede the existence of a 'primal theism' in Melanesia. He cites recent anthropological research among the Paiela of the Enga Province in the western highlands, who seem to have had a single, beneficent creator deity, though he sets against this the more typical findings of other anthropologists who can detect no trace of monotheism.[19] It seems that the priest-anthropologist Mantovani, whose starting-point is the sustained effort to grasp Melanesian religion phenomenologically, and the theology lecturer Garland, who bases himself on Augustine's classical analogy of the inner life of the Trinity with the human intellect and will, are talking past one another.

My own judgement would be that that the doctrine of the Trinity has been imposed on Melanesian religion from without, and therefore lacks a basis in experience in the Melanesian context. In more traditional terms, the 'immanent' Trinity as conceived by the classical theology of the West has been artificially superimposed on the 'economic' Trinity without the trouble being taken to verify just what form the divine economy takes in cultures as distinctive as those of the Pacific. It is as pointless to project their social structures onto the Christian God in a vain attempt to 'indigenise' the Trinity as it is to imagine that the traditional doctrine of the Trinity may be found reproduced in the radically different medium of Melanesian cultures. I am convinced that this failure to discover the true historical mediation of the Christian Trinity in Melanesian 'Life' is at the root of the wildfire growth of fundamentalism in present-day Melanesia as elsewhere in the Pacific.[20] The 'instant identity' offered by fundamentalism to uprooted islanders and disoriented Westerners alike, short-circuits the relationship of both to tradition, without which identity formation in a rapidly changing context cannot take place.

We are left with the question whether the doctrine of the Trinity has been enabling or oppressive in the Melanesian cultural and social context. The most prudent answer is that its real interaction with Melanesian religion is taking place in oral and ritual media largely inaccessible to Westerners and only imperfectly articulated as yet even by Melanesian theologians. One thing, however, is certain: authentic Christian faith, built on the credal affirmation of one God in three Persons, has taken a deep hold on the hearts and minds of Pacific Islanders everywhere in the region. As a result, the fruits of the Spirit (Gal 5:22) are already everywhere apparent, despite the weaknesses that flesh is heir to under the enormous destructive pressures of a too rapid modernisation and a spurious 'development'. This Christian leavening of Pacific life is evident in a vibrant ecumenism and a lived theology springing from traditions of hospitality and celebration, which make no small contribution to the integration of ecological and social concerns in the WCC's programme on Justice, Peace and the Integrity of Creation. It remains to be seen how our understanding of God will be further enriched by these peoples' encounter with the mystery of the Trinity.

Notes

1. For the early mission history of the Pacific see John Garrett, *To Live Among the Stars: Christian Origins in Oceania* (Geneva: WCC; Suva: University of the South Pacific, 1982); for a fuller treatment of Melanesia, Rufus Pech, 'The Acts of the Apostles in Papua New Guinea and Solomon Islands', in Brian Schwarz, ed., *An Introduction to Ministry in Melanesia* (Goroka: The Melanesian Institute, 1985) 17-71; and on the subsequent theological developments, John D'Arcy May, *Christus Initiator: Theologie im Pazifik* (Düsseldorf: Patmos, 1990).

2. The above data are drawn from the pioneering research of Rufus Pech, 'The Name of God in Melanesia', *Melanesian Journal of Theology* 1 (1985) 30-46, p. 31. Pech has given a masterly interpretation of the significance of the Manub-Kilibob myth, with all its linguistic and cultural ramifications, in his STM thesis *Myth, Dream and Drama – Shapers of a People's quest for Salvation* (Columbus, Ohio: Trinity Lutheran Seminary, 1989) now fortunately published as *Manub and Kilibob: Melanesian Models of Brotherhood* (Goroka: The Melanesian Institute, 1991). See also Theo Ahrens and Walter Hollenweger, *Volkschristentum und Volksreligion im Pazifik* (Frankfurt: Otto Lembeck, 1977). For an indigenous account of the secure possession of an active creator God by Melanesians, see Simon Apea, 'Footsteps of God in

Ialibu', J.D. May ed., *Living Theology in Melanesia: A Reader* (Goroka: The Melanesian Institute and The Melanesian Association of Theology Schools, 1985) 218 - 255.

3. Ennio Mantovani, 'Comparative Analysis of Cultures and Religions', in *id.* ed., *An Introduction to Melanesian Religion* (Goroka: The Melanesian Institute, 1984) 49- 86, p. 74.

4. cf. Gernot Fugmann, ed., *The Birth of An Indigenous Church: Letters, Reports and Documents of Lutheran Christians of Papua New Guinea* (Goroka: The Melanesian Institute, 1986).

5. Peter Lawrence, *Road Belong Cargo: A Study of the Cargo Movement in the Southern Madang District New Guinea* (Melbourne: Melbourne University Press, 1976[2]) 88. One of the most thorough and enlightening studies of a cargo cult is by Patrick V. Gesh, *Initiative and Initiation: A Cargo Cult-type Movement in the Sepik Against Its Background in Traditional Village Religion* (St Augustin: Anthropos-Institut, 1985). For the wider significance of the cults, see Theodor Ahrens, *Unterwegs nach der verlorenen Heimat. Studien zur Identitätsproblematik in Melanesien* (Erlangen: Verlag der Ev. -Luth. Mission, 1986). The first attempts at a theological evaluation were by G. Oosterwaal, *Modern Messianic Movements as a Theological and Missionary Challenge* (Elkhart, Ind.: Institute of Mennonite Studies, 1973) and John Strelan, *Search for Salvation: Studies in the History and Theology of Cargo Cults* (Adelaide: Lutheran Publishing House, 1977).

6. cf. Wendy Flannery, ed., *Religious Movements in Melanesia Today*, 3 vols (Goroka: The Melanesian Institute, 1983-84).

7. Joe Gaqurae, 'Indigenisation as Incarnation: The Concept of a Melanesian Christ', J.D. May, ed., *Living Theology in Melanesia*, 214, 216. For a fuller account of theological development in the Pacific along the lines developed here, see the final chapter of May, *Christus Initator*.

8. See my translation of Paliau's 'Makasol Kastam Kansol Stori' in May, ed., *Living Theology*, 31-43.

9. Anna Meigs, quoted by Ennio Mantovani, 'Is There a Biocosmic Religion? A Reply to Dr Garland', *Catalyst* 16 (1986) 352-366, pp. 360-61. I have commented further on the theological significance of this idea in May, *Christus Initiator*, Chapter 7.

10. Clear expositions of this rigorously consistent ethic have been given by Ennio Mantovani, 'Traditional Values and Ethics', Darrell Whiteman, ed., *An Introduction to Melanesian Cultures* (Goroka:

The Melanesian Institute, 1984) 195-212; and, 'Mipela Simbu! The Pig Festival and Simbu Identity', Victor C. Hayes, ed., *Identity Issues and World Religions* (Adelaide: Australian Association for the Study of Religions, 1986). Garry Trompf, *Melanesian Religion* (Cambridge: Cambridge University Press, 1991) Chapter 3, places the ethic of *payback* in the overall context of Melanesian religion.

11. Christopher Garland, 'Is Traditional Religion in Papua New Guinea Theistic?', *Catalyst* 16 (1986) 127-145, 127.

12. Garland, 'Traditional Religion', 130.

13. Ibid, 133

14. Ibid, 135-36.

15. Ennio Mantovani, 'Is there a Biocosmic Religion?', 352. See also J.D. May, 'The Prospects of Melanesian Theology', *Catalyst* 14 (1984) 290-301, and the inaugural issue of the *Melanesian Journal of Theology*, 1 (1985) 10-82.

16. Mantovani, 'Is there a Biocosmic Religion?', 353.

17. Ibid, 356.

18. Ibid.

19. Ibid., 358-361.

20. cf. John D'Arcy May, *Christian Fundamentalism and Melanesian Identity* (Goroka: The Melanesian Institute Occasional Paper No. 3, 1986). Dr. Manfred Ernst, based at Pacific Theological College in Suva, Fiji, is currently undertaking a comprehensive study of 'rapidly growing religious groups' throughout the Pacific (but excluding Papua New Guinea).

CHAPTER SEVENTEEN

The Christian God And Allah

Redmond Fitzmaurice

Islamic Monotheism

The Islamic profession of faith (the *shahadah*) that there is no god but Allah (*the* God) and that Muhammad is the Messenger of *Allah*, is an assertion of the radical oneness of God. It is important to note at the very beginning that the term *Allah* is not an exclusively Islamic term; it is the common Arabic term for God which was, and is, used by Arabic-speaking Jews and Christians. If the central Islamic assertion is that God is One, then the great sin in Islam is *shirk* – polytheism or idolatry. The root meaning of *shirk* is to 'bring together', to 'associate', or to 'participate in'. The sin of *shirk*, then, is to attribute divinity to any other reality apart from God; to multiply gods, or to put any other being on the same level as God. It is from the same root as *shirk* that we get the Quranic word for an idolater – *mushrik*. So in Islam there is this polar opposition between *tawhid*, (the dogma of the utter unity of God) and *shirk* (the sin of multiplying gods or associating other beings with God).

It is sometimes assumed that, because Islam is chronologically post-Christian, it is essentially a reaction to or a development of the Christian understanding of God. This is not a useful way to approach Islam. In my opinion, it is better to think of Islam as a pre-Christian phenomenon. Islam is a movement from polytheism or henotheism (the concept of one *supreme* god which would allow for subordinate divinities) to a very rigorous monotheism. Certainly when Muhammad began his prophetic preaching (c.610AD), the concept of monotheism, or at least of a supreme god, was already present among the Arabs of the peninsula. The Qur'an challenges the pagan Arabs:

> If thou askest them, 'Who created the heavens and the earth, and subjected the sun and the moon?' they will say 'Allah'. If thou askest them, 'Who sends down out of the heavens water

> and wherewith revives the earth after it is dead?' they will say 'Allah'. (Qur'an 31:24)

In another place[1] the pagan Arabs are accused of only calling on *Allah* when they are in extreme distress and of then forgetting about him. Other evidence that the notion of *Allah* as the supreme God was already present to the Arabs is found in the fact that it had entered into personal names. Muhammad's own father was called *Abdallah* – 'servant of God'.

However, the notion of one supreme God was not the predominant one in pre-Islamic times. In the time of *jahiliyya* (of 'ignorance'), as that era is known in the Islamic tradition, the common religion seems to have been a primitive animism in which rocks, trees and wells were of special significance and considered to be inhabited by good or bad spirits, known as *jinn*. These had to be propitiated. There were also more localised, named deities which were often represented by crude figures or stones. In the locality of Mecca three female deities were worshipped – *al-Lat* (the feminine form of *Allah*), *al-Uzza*, and *al-Manat*. These three goddesses were known as *Banat Allah* – the 'daughters of Allah' and are mentioned in the Qur'an.[2] It was against this pagan practice of approaching *Allah* through sub-gods (his 'daughters' or maybe even his 'sons') that the second most important *surah*, or chapter, of the Qur'an was proclaimed.[3]

> Say: 'He is God, One God, the Everlasting Refuge, who has not begotten, and has not been begotten, and equal to Him is not any one.' (Qur'an 112)

This early Meccan *surah* was certainly first directed against the Arabs of the *jahiliyya* and their worship of the offspring of *Allah*. However, at a later date when Muhammad heard Christians refer to God as 'Father', and to Jesus as the 'Son of God', these words were then addressed to them. The Christian language and terminology regarding Trinity and Incarnation were heard in terms of the pagan Arab notion of the *Banat Allah* and this subsequently coloured the whole debate.

The great achievement of Muhammad was that he made the originally somewhat peripheral notion of *Allah* – the One unique God – central in his preaching so that ultimately it became the central truth of the faith of his followers. The vast majority of the Arabs of the peninsula (ultimately all of them) became Muslims; one people worshipping One God. This created a unity and an energy which bore fruit after the death of the Prophet in the success of the Arab conquests and the establishing of Islam as a world culture and civilisation which came to dominate the eastern Mediterranean, Iraq, Iran, India and was powerfully present in black Africa and south east Asia.

The Encounter with Christianity

Eastern Christian and later medieval Latin polemic assumed that Muhammad's core notion of God – his central religious conviction – came from contact with Christianity. The assumption was that Muhammad, consciously or unconsciously, created Islam from elements of the two great biblical religions. An examination of the earliest traditions regarding the religious crisis which affected Muhammad when he was about forty years old, and of the experiences he had when he went alone into the mountains above Mecca, do not support that contention.[4] The evidence of the earliest *surahs* of the Qur'an is that for Muhammad the experience and conviction of the utter oneness of God was totally original, overwhelming and personal. In the chronologically earliest sections of the Qur'an these experiences are expressed in striking, vivid images which are quite distinct from the images and language of the Bible. It was only later, with the growing assurance that the revelation he had received was identical with that formerly given to the Jewish and Christian communities, that the revelations begin to be expressed in language more familiar to us from the Bible. It was then that the Hebrew patriarchs and Jesus began to be spoken of as forerunners of Muhammad; prophets who had proclaimed the same message and suffered the same trials.

From the fact that so many biblical figures are mentioned in the Qur'an (e.g. Adam, Noah, Abraham, Ishmael, Moses, Jesus, and Mary) it is clear that there must have been a substantial Jewish and Christian presence in Arabia in pre-Islamic times. The stories must have been current, otherwise the preaching and revelations would not have been intelligible or effective. Yet though the biblical stories were circulating, it is certain that there was no Arabic translation of the Jewish or Christian scriptures in existence before the coming of Islam. They were passed on verbally. Encouraged by these stories, Muhammad first approached Jews and Christians with the conviction that the message they had received was identical with the one he was proclaiming. So in an early Meccan revelation, Muslims are advised that if they have any difficulties interpreting the Word of God they should consult the Jews and the Christians.[5] The Muslim conviction was, and is, that the original revelation given to Moses in the *tawrah* (Torah) and that given to Jesus in the *injil* (Gospel) were essentially in harmony with the revelation given to Muhammad in the Qur'an because they all came from the one primordial and eternal source in God. So we read:

> Dispute not with the People of the Book [i.e. Jews and Christians] save in the fairer manner, except for those of them who do wrong; and say, 'We believe in what has been sent down to us, and what has been sent down to you; our God and your God is One, and to Him we have surrendered.' (Qur'an 29:45)

Afterwards, when he discovered that the Jews and Christians did not accept him as the definitive prophet sent by God to complete the work of divine revelation, we find the Qur'an reaching back behind both of these traditions to Abraham who preceded Moses and Jesus.

> No, Abraham in truth was not a Jew, neither a Christian, but he was a Muslim and one of pure faith (*hanif*), certainly he was not one of the idolaters. (Qur'an 6:79)

The term *hanif* is an appeal to a claimed earlier true Arab monotheism which in the Muslim understanding was considered to be independent of both Judaism and Christianity

Islam differs from the other great non-Christian world religions in that it is chronologically post-Christian and in that it has taken a definite stance with regard to central Christian dogmas. The Qur'an eventually came to the conclusion that the majority of Christians have distorted the revelation they received from God through Jesus Son of Mary and set out to correct what it saw as the errors of Christians. As already stated, these 'errors' are seen and judged in terms of pre-Islamic polytheism – as another example of attributing sons and daughters to *Allah*. To correct this the Qur'an fashions a Quranic Jesus; one who differs in essentials from the Christ of Christian faith. The main areas of difficulty are the doctrines of the Incarnation and the Trinity.

In the Qur'an Jesus is certainly recognised as a major prophet. However, it is insisted that Jesus is only a human being – that he cannot be called the 'Son of God'.

> Truly, the likeness of Jesus in God's sight is as the likeness of Adam; he created him out of dust then he said to him 'Be', and he was. (Qur'an 3:52)

> They say the All-Merciful has taken to himself a son...the heaven would almost be rent, the earth split, the mountains come crashing down...It is not fitting for the All-Merciful to take a son. (Qur'an 19:88-92)

Behind this utter rejection in the Qur'an of the title 'Son of God' is an understanding of the divine Incarnation that at some point in time the Almighty acquired or 'adopted' a human being as his son. This is a primary meaning of the verb *ittakhadha* in the above *surah* v.91.[6] Most horribly, for Muslims, this son is considered to be the fruit of carnal intercourse with Mary. This understanding is not explicit in the Qur'an but did emerge in later polemical debates between Muslims and Christians. However, the Qur'an in one place does seem to understand the Trinity as consisting of *Allah*, Mary and Jesus – father, mother and child. This is implied in the rhetorical question: 'And when God said, 'O Jesus, Son of Mary, didst thou say unto men, "Take me and my mother as gods apart from God?"' (Qur'an 5:116). The answer is of course 'No'.

It need not be assumed that these misunderstandings of the orthodox Christian doctrine of the Incarnation and the Trinity are exclusively of Muslim origin. They may well have come from Christian sources. There may have been Monophysite or even Syrian-Semitic Christians who were genuinely shocked by or misunderstood the subtleties of these Christian dogmas as they were being defined in councils by Greek Byzantine theologians.[7] Perhaps the idea of Mary being part of the Trinity originated with a Nestorian attack on the council of Ephesus and the title it gave Mary of *Theotokos* – 'mother of God'. The Qur'an does not say that these views were held by all Christians – but at least by some. In passing it is interesting to note how central trinitarian terms such as 'Word' and 'Spirit' are found in the text of the Qur'an without their Christian significance being acknowledged or accepted.

> People of the Book, go not beyond the bounds in your religion, and say not as to God but the truth. The Messiah, Jesus, Son of Mary, was only the Messenger of God, and his Word that he committed to Mary, and a Spirit from him. So believe in God and his messengers, and say not 'Three'. Refrain; it is better for you. God is only one God. Glory be to Him that he should have a son! (Qur'an 4:169-170)[8]

In this quotation we touch on the difficulty, ambiguity and frustration of Christians and Muslims entering into a theological dialogue. Islam is so resistant to anything that in any way infringes the transcendent Oneness and uniqueness of God that it is almost impossible for the majority of Muslims even to begin to enter with understanding into the specifically Christian dogmas of the Trinity and of the mystery that 'God was in Christ reconciling the world to himself' (2 Cor 5:19), because they cannot see how, as Christians claim, these doctrines can be reconciled with the core Muslim assertion that there is no God but *Allah*. The result is that in discussions with most ordinary Muslims these questions have to be bracketed – left aside for the time being – until the partners in dialogue have reached a much more profound level of trust and understanding. To broach these topics too soon is to end up in unpleasant and unproductive wrangling. We have first to rest together in contemplation of God as the one source of all being, guidance and ultimate reward. In this we agree.

Notes

1. Qur'an 10:23-24.
2. Qur'an 53:20.
3. The most important *surah* of the Qur'an is undoubtedly the opening one – *Surah al-Fatihah*.
4. cf. W.Montgomery Watt, *Muhammad at Mecca* (Oxford: OUP, 1953) 40-41.
5. cf. Qur'an 10:94.
6. cf. Kenneth Cragg, *The Arab Christian: a History in the Middle East* (London: 1992) 48, footnote 1.

7. There is a whole literature on Jesus in the Qur'an. Geoffrey Parrinder, *Jesus in the Quran* (London: 1965). W.Montgomery Watt, 'The Christianity criticised in the Qur'an', *The Muslim World*, vol 57 (1967) 197-201. Heilki Raisanen, 'The Portrait of Jesus in the Qur'an: Reflections of a Biblical Scholar', *The Muslim World*, vol 70 (1980) 122-133.
8. A Muslim scholar, Ali Merad, has analysed the terms applied to Jesus in the Qur'an and come to the conclusion that there is something very special about them which the Muslim tradition has not faced up to. While not accepting the Christian claims to the divinity of Jesus, he does concede that Jesus is a uniquely special figure in the Qur'an. cf. 'Christ According to the Qur'an', *Encounter*, n.69, published by the Pontifical Institute for Arabic and Islamic Studies (P.I.S.A.I,), Rome.

Contributors

VINCENT BRÜMMER is Professor of Theology, University of Utrecht, The Netherlands.

JAMES M. BYRNE lectures in Systematic Theology, Trinity College, Dublin.

GABRIEL DALY is Lecturer in Systematic Theology, Trinity College, Dublin.

JOHN D'ARCY MAY lectures in Interfaith Dialogue and Social Ethics, Irish School of Ecumenics.

REDMOND FITZMAURICE lectures in Islam, Milltown Park Institute, Dublin, and is a member of the Currach Ecumenical Community, Belfast.

SEAN FREYNE is Professor of Theology, Trinity College, Dublin.

WERNER G. JEANROND is Senior Lecturer in Systematic Theology, Trinity College, Dublin.

URSULA KING is Professor of Theology, University of Bristol.

ANN LOADES is Reader in Theology, University of Durham.

JAMES P. MACKEY is Challoner Professor of Theology, University of Edinburgh.

JANET MARTIN SOSKICE is Lecturer in Divinity, University of Cambridge.

ANDREW MAYES is Erasmus Smith's Professor of Hebrew, Trinity College, Dublin.

JÜRGEN MOLTMANN is Professor of Systematic Theology, University of Tübingen, Germany.

CHRISTOPH SCHWÖBEL is Professor of Theology, University of Kiel, Germany.

PAUL SURLIS is Associate Professor of Theology, St John's University, New York.

DAVID TRACY is Andrew Thomas Greely and Grace McNichols Greely Distinguished Service Professor of Roman Catholic Studies, University of Chicago Divinity School.

ROWAN WILLIAMS, formerly Lady Margaret Professor of Divinity, Oxford University, is now the Bishop of Monmouth.